The *Integrity* Effect

The *Integrity* Effect

Melissa Joy Jonsson

HEART-FIELD PRODUCTIONS

Published by Heart-Field Productions Inc.
Seattle, WA 98136
info@mjoyheartfield.com

21 20 19 18 17   1 2 3 4 5

ISBN: 978-0-9986565-1-9 (Kindle)
ISBN: 978-0-9986565-2-6 (ebk)
ISBN: 978-0-9986565-0-2 (pbk)

Library of Congress Control Number: 2017901231

Cover and page design by Holly Monteith

This book is dedicated to my dear friend Greta, who knowingly (and unknowingly) embodies the principles of the Integrity Effect. Thank you for first seeing within me a potential I had yet to recognize.

<><><>

To the many brave Lion Hearts in my life, for showing me love's eternal, consistent, and transformative nature. Love never goes anywhere. Only circumstances change.

<><><>

Finally, special appreciation to my Cabo family, who supported me (and playfully distracted me) throughout the writing of this book. Thank you for reasons that defy logic and delight my heart.

Contents

◇◇◇◇◇◇

Introduction

You already are what you wish to become.

Have you ever looked at an old picture of yourself and wondered how your life might have played out differently if only you had known then what you know now? Perhaps you may have told yourself that who you were then has enabled you to become who you are today?

Or perhaps someone else told you that prior experiences, no matter how positive or painful, were necessary, as they helped shape you into the person you are today? Or maybe you can't even relate to that person you once were in the distant or not-so-distant past?

Perhaps old photos and memories of earlier times are so painful that they are stored away in a mental and emotional vault, and you have thrown away the key or forgotten the combination?

While writing this book, I came across my senior portrait from high school. The picture was a typical high school photo, somewhat dated by the ridiculous 1980s fashion and hairstyle of that particular genre. As with many youthful photos, there appeared an essence of innocence, hope, beauty, and potential.

While glancing at this snapshot in time, a reflection of an earlier version of myself, I too wondered what my life would have been like if I (consciously) had known then what I (seem) to know now. As I looked at the photo, instantly my mind was flooded by memories of my life at that time.

I had just been accepted to a university of choice, played goalie on an all-star varsity soccer team, and was in (teen) love with my high school sweetheart. According to other people's standards, I appeared to be on the path to great success. It seemed like I had it all.

But as my present self looked at the picture, into the eyes of the earlier me, I was haunted by the gap between how I genuinely felt about myself at that time and the way my life appeared. Earlier me was so disconnected from myself, my body, my sense of source, and others. I felt disconnected from virtually everything. My own light was muted and dimmed just to allegedly fit in.

Only a few years prior to that picture being taken, my life had looked dramatically different, and so had I. I had been more than fifty pounds overweight, had a buzz hair-cut bleached platinum white, and been using illicit and prescription drugs as well as alcohol, while failing school due to chronic absenteeism. Through this challenging time of self-avoidance and self-loathing, I was somehow aware that I was on a path that could potentially limit my future options. I was afraid that if I did not make different choices, I would end up destitute, or maybe even dead. I was miserable, and I was scared.

But something inside me knew I was destined for something more. I had a knowing without knowing how I knew— that I could change my trajectory, change my choices, and therefore change my life. Although I was afraid, I resolved to get my act together. I committed to exercising and eating healthily, stopped all drug and alcohol use, and began regularly attending classes at school. I decided to show up for my life.

Within six months, I had lost all the extra weight, was totally sober, and had earned a straight-A report card.

Indeed, I had gotten my act together. My fear had served me well. Yet, as I looked retrospectively into the eyes of my younger me in the photo, I realized (as I somehow knew then) that I was only graduating to a different act—a portrayal that enabled me to hang with the popular crowd, date a varsity football player, and attend a coveted university. I had my act together . . . but I didn't feel authentic. Beneath my mask, my persona, and my scripted map, I had no idea who I was. I was showing up for what was expected of me. I was aware of a gap between the real me inside and the me I was projecting to the rest of the world. Inside I felt so empty, void of self-love and inner trust, and I was still filled with fear.

Soon thereafter, my weight loss program morphed into a full-blown, diagnosed eating disorder. My sobriety and studiousness became new forms of compulsive habits, addictions unto themselves that were distractions from a chronic feeling of not being OK with myself. I reasoned that I had things *under control*. And control indeed had me. I was still gripped with fear. Yet, beneath my fear was an awareness that I didn't feel self-love. I was starving for self-affection and was desperately trying to control my reality to feel safe.

As l look back now, I can see how confused I was, running distorted societal, cultural, and family programs, expectations promising happiness, abundance, and the good life. But I was not living on my terms, according to the true callings of my heart. I didn't even know what *heart-terms* meant.

If only I knew then what I know now, that I already was what I wished to become—that there already existed within me seeds of love's completion and everything I needed to know to live a truly authentic life. If only I had known and trusted that the true me, found within my heart, could map to and match a projected identity-me without. They could exist together cohesively as one and the same.

This cohesiveness is possible for all of us. This cohesiveness as self-love is possible for you.

If only I had known then what you can soon discover in this book—that the self-love, authenticity, and integrity that I craved was already within me, waiting to emerge. If only I knew that within the field of my heart were all the key codes necessary to live an extraordinary life . . . on my terms. If only I had known how to access this inner wisdom, how much self-abuse, recrimination, judgment, fear, and manipulation could I have avoided? What choices would I have made differently if I had loved myself and been my own best friend?

Perhaps you may wonder this, too, not just retrospectively, but now. What choices might you make differently *now* if you genuinely loved and appreciated yourself?

What if the gap between who you truly are and how you have been conditioned to behave (be-have/act) could close? What if this gap could close between your inner self and your outer reality, and you could open to your own True Authentic Magnificence? This is possible for and available to everyone through the teachings shared throughout *The Integrity Effect.*

Although hindsight is often enlightening, there is little value in looking back to the past with regret. However, there is great value in recognizing that we perhaps did the best we could at the time, equipped with the information and resources we had during those experiences. But what if we could have *more* information now that could change even how we relate to past experiences? More importantly, what if this information could be leveraged to significantly alter our current lives and future possibilities? This is indeed probable by applying the principles shared within the pages of this book. We can reconfigure life experiences in all directions.

If I had known back then that I would eventually become a public speaker, life transformational seminar instructor, author of multiple books, and personal empowerment coach to thousands of people around the world, I would have scoffed incredulously at the notion. That wasn't me, I would have reasoned. I could never stand up confidently in front of hundreds of people and spontaneously and vulnerably speak for several days at a time, healing and transforming lives as I have healed and transformed my own. And yet, this is exactly what I do and have done so successfully for many years.

Indeed, a significant gap of time has elapsed between the teenager in that photo and the person into whom I have evolved today. That gap in time was spent earning a degree in psychology, attending business school, cultivating a career in the pharmaceutical industry for more than a decade, and developing workaholic behaviors to boot.

This was followed by quitting my lucrative career, packing up all my belongings, and placing them in storage so I could move to Hawaii (to do nothing but sit on the beach and sell flower leis). One year later, I returned to all my "stuff" and also to my familiar, reliable, and safe pharmaceutical career.

I moved twenty-three times in fifteen years. Amid these changes, I cultivated new addictions and resumed old ones. I resigned again with finality from the pharmaceutical industry, got married, and moved again. I then divorced and moved again. Movement seemed like a solution that would help me. Yet, nothing could move (or fill) the void of emptiness I consistently felt within. I kept creating external changes in the hope that I would feel OK. Yet, wherever we go, there we are.

Ultimately, I was seeking to love and feel better about myself. Perhaps you can relate? Though the details of our life experiences, choices, and addictions may differ, maybe you have been on the move, looking for love in all the wrong places?

In retrospect, I recognize that I went through a series of dramatic acts that led to my unique story. But my story is now history (or "her story," as I like to say), as today I am not who I thought I used to be. And yet, who I used to *really* be is still who I am now—love and limitless potential. This never changes, no matter what. I just didn't realize this. I now know I am love and limitless potential and that all is possible from the field of the heart. *We all are love and limitless potential.* All is possible from the field of the heart.

I have become my own best friend, embracing my True Authentic Self and living according to the volition of my heart. I live and love via the principles of the Integrity Effect and teach others to do the same, in their own unique manner.

But my story is not what this book is about.

This book is about You (and me) in the shared WE experience. This book is about the power of living fully from our hearts, coupled with our minds, to experience the joy and power of the Integrity Effect.

Is it *really* true that who we thought we were in the past made us who we are today? Is it *really* true that who we were defines us now? Perhaps these are just stories we tell ourselves to justify our experiences? Perhaps these are just stories that perpetuate our stories?

Stories are purposeful, as they help us organize our experiences. They are like maps we follow to make sense of our lives. We may extract meaning out of a collection of seemingly random events. Yet, rigid adherence to stories keeps us shackled to the perceived experiences as though they are still happening now. We are not our stories.

Consider that who we are is so much more than the sum of our stories and experiences. When we move beyond the stories that have defined us, into the heart of our inherent potential, we can align our lives to an inner truth and clarity to consistently access True Authentic Power, joy, and fulfillment.

Our stories are programs that we run over and over again in our minds like old recordings stuck on perpetual play. These fragments of partially woven narratives can form the tapestry for our experiences. However, we can create new programs, new tapestries, and new maps to follow through the various changing terrains of our lives. When we move fully into our hearts, we move beyond our stories and recognize our stories for what they are, simply experiences as placeholders in our awareness.

To some extent, I have always been adept at making changes. Perhaps we all are. Some consider me a change master. What I have learned along the way, through trials and distinctions, is that until we change how we relate to ourselves, joy and genuine fulfillment will perpetually elude us. More importantly, I have discovered that loving self and living wholly in integrity are not really difficult. In fact, both self-love and integrity are facets of our natural state. We can all do this. We can all love ourselves.

It is not so much that we need to change into something different to experience self-love. Instead, we simply need to stop not allowing love to exist from within us. We just need to stop not being who we truly are, if only we knew how. The Integrity Effect will light the way.

Consider that embracing authenticity as integrity and self-love is possible no matter where we may find ourselves in our individual and shared human journey. We all deserve to access this natural state of joy, love, and integrity. For this reason, I have mapped the terminology and processes that have worked for me and included them in this book. These principles have been successfully taught to thousands of people around the world through the evolutionary M-Joy teachings.

Through my extensive experience as a life transformational seminar instructor and empowerment coach, I have had the privilege of interacting with and helping tens of thousands of students, groups, clients, and even strangers all around the world transform their relationships to themselves and therefore transform their relationships to . . . everything.

This unique framework and language consistently enable people from all walks of life to embrace their True Authentic Self, to experience self-love and the joy of living with authenticity as integrity. These benefits affect individuals and the collective alike and are what I refer to as the *Integ-*

rity Effect. This is available to you within the pages of this book.

As a leading authority since 2008 on the physics of heart-centered awareness and interactive reality creation, I have developed a unique system of teachings known as M-Joy that encodes for these principles and are shared herein.

Throughout this book, you will discover how to PLAY the change game from the inside out, on your own heart-terms. With joy. In-Joy. You are joy. We are joy. M-Joy teaches a language and framework of completion, terminology where self-love is the new normal.

This book will change you simply by reading it. Just read. The Integrity Effect will close the gap between your perceived limitations and your innate limitless potential. You do not need to know the physics (or science) to close the gap between who you think you are and who you truly are. This book, though it does not include physics, encodes for the physics of sustainable transformation that can occur instantly or along the continuum of time.

In the same manner that you do not need to know how electricity functions to flip a switch and light up a room, you do not need to know the physics of integrity to switch off your programs of confusion and shine your light as coherency and congruency in action.

All that is required to derive tremendous benefit from this book is curiosity and a willingness to PLAY. This book is a journey into you and will provide powerful tools to create new maps for joy, fulfillment, and True Authentic Power through the Integrity Effect.

Words are carrier waves for transformation. As you read this book, the encoded words will support you in moving out of old, limiting programs and paradigms into new, expansive possibilities, ready to actualize as experience. This book will carry you into an embodied experience of self-love, connection, and completion. Just read and transform into the truth of your essential self, your awesome self, your True Authentic Self.

For those who like to do, who may want to practice what is being shared, there is an abundance of Practical Play offered in many chapters. These are fun, easy, and empowering exercises that will assist anyone in implementing the experience of self-love and authenticity in action. The Integrity Effect can be enhanced through consistent Practical Play that can re-create the story lines scripting our reality.

Come join me on a journey into the WE experience, where, together, we will create new maps for navigating toward our inherent magnificence. The Integrity Effect is how we Play It Forward to benefit ourselves and the collective alike. Come join me as we experience together the Integrity Effect. Just choose to read and PLAY.

—*Melissa Joy*

1

Moving into the Gap

We create our own reality.

This is a popular meme circulating through the collective consciousness that says we create our own reality. Pursuant to this notion is the idea that we are each responsible for everything that happens to us and around us.

Everything? Does this mean if a volcano erupts in Hawaii, we are personally responsible for the occurrence? Or if a relative commits suicide, or our child dies, that we somehow (consciously or unconsciously) created that choice as experience?

What if a war occurs among nations with opposing ideologies; are we creating that reality from the remote privacy of our living rooms? What if, during an economic downturn, we are laid off from a company we loved, in which we had outstanding performance reviews consistently every year? Did we create that reality too?

The concept that "we create our own reality" seems a little oversimplified and, to a lesser degree, egocentric. Certainly we are not the center and instigator of all circumstances in our reality? Yet the notion that we create our own reality seems to imply that this is the case.

This is an easy idea to accept when things go our way. We are very receptive to being responsible for our successes. Some may consider abundance and accomplishments to be a function of luck, skill, or perhaps tenacity, but regardless of what we call our Midas touch, we have no problem being responsible for making reality happen.

But what about when things do not go our way? What then?

Proponents of the Law of Attraction imply that we create our own reality by attracting what we focus on. This attraction is magnetized by our own resonant energy, sometimes called frequency. Presumably, when what we focus on and expect from our minds (consciously) does not match our actual frequency or energy (often unconsciously), we wind up not getting what we expected. So they say we are still creating our reality even if what we create ends up being what we think we do not want.

So if we are totally creating our reality, it seems we would be able to create a reality where our unconscious energy or vibration does not cancel out what we focus on, intend, or desire.

Some might offer that reality doesn't always go our way and challenges occur because our souls agree to have certain experiences before we incarnate. Well, then, that would imply that we do not necessarily have free will, the freedom of choice. And if we are creating our own reality according to an agreed upon preconceived soul blueprint, then through free will as choice, we would also be free to change that blueprint as creators of our reality.

Reality is not that simple.

We do not really create our own reality. Not entirely.

Consider that the idea that we create our own reality is perhaps not entirely true, or untrue, but is potentially useful, as the belief can help us to feel occasionally empowered.

However rigid an adherence to this notion we create, our own reality may result in feelings of failure and self-condemnation when things do not seem to go our way as intended.

Perhaps no matter how hard we may try; no matter how positive our thinking, how strong our beliefs, or how consistent our actions; regardless of how many times we may "get in the vortex" or follow the Law of Attraction, we encounter distractions and destructions that spin us in a direction bearing little resemblance to what we had envisioned for ourselves.

"What are we doing wrong?" we may ask. Do we need another book, seminar, or coaching session to tell us what we have yet to figure out? What is the secret, and why is the universe allegedly keeping it from us?

Indeed, maintaining awareness that we create our own reality does empower us to make changes in our lives. If our thoughts, beliefs, and choices are creating our circumstances, then conceivably we can change our thoughts, beliefs, and choices to create different circumstances and experiences.

However, is reality really this simple? Or is there truly more to interactive reality creation than our own individual notions, emotions, energy, and actions?

Party of Experience

Perhaps it is not so much that we create our own reality as it is that we participate in creating and interacting with our individual and shared realities. We actively engage in the co-creative process consciously (and often unconsciously), and we have the power to choose how we react, respond, and relate to what seems to be happening as reality. We create our experience of reality.

When we change how we relate to our reality, through our inner actions and interactions, then we indeed change our personal and often shared perceived experiences. We may not change the immediate outward circumstances, but when we change how we relate to our circumstances, there is a ripple effect that influences everything.

Reality of WE Experience

Furthermore, consider that our experience of reality is more than the sole result of individual creative impulses; rather, reality is a function of a complex interplay of interconnected variables. Our individual choices, as well as the choices of others, are inexorably woven together in an interdependent synergy that creates a diverse tapestry of experiences. Our individual experiences are entangled with everyone else's individual experiences. Reality includes all these experiences.

Everything in reality is in relation to . . . itself. Everything is also *You in relation to . . . everything*. Your own experience of reality is based on where you resonate and how you connect with and relate to reality. Your projections, reflections, and connections continually serve as filters, mirrors, and windows into realms of individual and collective experiences.

What if we do create our own reality and there are also invariably circumstances that occur beyond our locus of control? How do we reconcile this perceived disparity into empowered forms of creating and relating to ourselves, others, and life in general? How do we change up external circumstances that seem to involve factors beyond our immediate grasp?

Language of the Heart

One of the most important tools for making distinctions and relating to our reality is language. Through the use of language, we categorize, identify, and name our experiences. Ultimately, we perceive the world according to our language.

Our experience of reality is largely a function of the language we use to describe and reference reality.

As human beings, when we experience something new and unfamiliar, our minds will perform a few automatic activities. Our minds may ask, "What is this I am experiencing? How can I label and organize this *unknown* in my awareness?" To do this, our minds will compare and contrast the experience: "This is like something I already know, so this must be that," or "This is not like something I already know, so this isn't that." Or our minds will simply dismiss the experience from reality because the experience is beyond the mind's limited perceptual filters.

Words are carrier waves that connect us to both the seen and unseen aspects of our reality. We can't see love, but we have an innate feeling for what it is. We can also experience the effects of love in myriad ways. The word *love* enables us to connect to and relate to the experience of love even though the word *love* is not the experience. The word *love* represents the experience.

Through language, we relate to our reality. Yet language as a symbolic representation of reality can, by its very nature, fragment our consciousness and, consequently, fragment the experience of ourselves and our reality. Thus our experience of reality is often limited by virtue of the language we are using.

What if there were a language for organizing reality where we could relate to reality and ourselves not from a framework of segregation and compartmentalization but from a framework of completion? What if this language could describe a terrain innate to everyone if only there were a way to map it? What if this new language enabled people to expand beyond their perceptual biases and programmed ways of navigating through the world, to experience the truth of their own unity and completion? What if this language could open anyone to the power and joy of the Integrity Effect?

The Integrity Effect and the constructs utilized to organize reality occur via a new language for relating to all experiences of reality from the heart–mind of completion. This language also provides coordinates for creating new maps to navigate through current changing landscapes. These maps reflect on our inherent love and unbounded potential no matter what has happened, may be happening, or is yet to occur. This integrative language of heart-centered awareness coupled with the power of congruent choices creates indelible imprints, heart-prints that pave the way for the Integrity Effect to ripple into our personal and collective realities.

The Integrity Effect

How do we bridge the perceived gap between where we are in our current experiences and where we want to be as individuals, within our families, in our work dynamics, and among the collective global community?

The answers lie not in minding the gap such that the gap becomes bigger, because in many cases, what we focus on will grow, and we will end up getting more of what we do not want. Rather, answers rest in *moving into the gap,* integrating who we think we are with who we truly are. We move into the gap by embodying the integrity of our True Authentic Self. The answer rests in the Integrity Effect.

The Integrity Effect is noticed and experienced through the embodiment of heart-centered awareness. As a result of living from the heart in a space of coherency, making congruent choices that are aligned with the wisdom of the heart, we experience the beneficial ripple effect of symmetric physics expressing through proportional unity and completion. When we live from our hearts, connected to our True Authentic Self, there is no gap. There is only connection.

Moving into Concrescence

The Integrity Effect fosters concrescence. *Concrescence* is defined as the growing together and merging of like or unlike separate parts or particles.[1] When we embody integrity as individuals, we experience concrescence as unity and connection within ourselves. Consequently, we are able to relate to others (and all of reality) through perceptual filters of unity rather than of separation and division.

The Integrity Effect at the level of the individual enables concrescence to begin to occur at the level of the collective consciousness. It begins with us. The Integrity Effect begins with you and me in the WE experience.

Integrity is not some external standard that we must strive toward, like a moving target that perpetually evades our reach. Integrity is also not an earned award, nor is it a moral standard to follow, although integrity can foster morals. Integrity is not found outside ourselves; rather, integrity emanates from within our hearts and is reflected without via the unfolding of corresponding circumstances.

Integrity is what permits our unique soul signature to emerge from heart to sole, as we step forth into the world one moment and movement at a time. Integrity requires consistent choices for sustainability.

Though integrity is a substance that cannot be seen or touched, like a chair can be, the essence of integrity emerges invisibly and undivided from the seat of our soul, creating an indelible imprint—a coherency that IS reflected in all matters. We can choose integrity. Just choose.

Containers for Integrity

Words, deeds, and actions are all energetic containers for the essence of integrity to flow. Integrity is the skin of the soul, our largest organ and interface (inner-face), which breathes life into all endeavors.

When integrity is congested by confusion, deception, or manipulation, the flow of integrity is obstructed in all systems of inner actions and interactions. Integrity is not a barrier; rather, integrity is a carrier wave to bare what is raw and authentic in the heart-soul of our being. Integrity opens us to our truth, a song for the soul's transmission of love—love that transmutes and transforms everything.

Integrity cannot be compartmentalized, no matter how many mental lies are told. When integrity is compromised, the broken promise to self reverberates into the eternal soul.

Broken integrity creates wounds that lie before us. Initially the wounds may be only scratches or scuffs we may overlook, mask, or cover by a bandage. Left unattended without authentic awareness, the wounds will fester, bleed, and infect all organizations of the interconnected systems of reality.

What once was hidden by a bandage of protection may bondage the soul's True Authentic Expression. Life circumstances will present like salt thrown in the wound to beckon our attention.

Through our hearts, we can air the wounds with the breath of honesty, inspired by integrity. This loving action will flow directly to the hemorrhage and heal the soul, restoring cohesiveness by providing wounds with the necessary ingredients to mend what once was severed.

We can allow the organ of integrity to orchestrate harmonic symphonies in all aspects of life with ease as grace. Love is integrity and can end all self-betrayal. Love as integrity is loyalty to the soul.

Defining Integrity

Integrity is deeply personal to everyone and yet transpersonal in that it affects everyone. Integrity may mean something different to everyone, depending upon personal thoughts and beliefs. It is not important that we be on the same page with respect to defining integrity. What is important is that you discover the essence of integrity that already exists within your heart.

Nonetheless, the integrity I am describing is an energetic integrity, centered in the heart, which radiates through congruent choices and actions, reflected in observable matters of everyday reality. Integrity includes a facet of transparency.

At the time this book is being written, there are no technological tools to measure energetic integrity. We can observe the effects of embodying integrity. We can also sense integrity like we may notice the presence of light in a dark room. We are attracted to the radiating essence of integrity as the light of life.

However, simply because we can't measure energetic integrity doesn't mean it doesn't exist and can't eventually be captured scientifically as an observable and measurable phenomenon.

As heart coherence can now be measured through electromagnetic tools, evidenced through HeartMath Institute research, I suspect the energetics of the Integrity Effect will also someday be measurable too.

Simply because energetic integrity may not yet be measurable does not mean it does not exist, for integrity as an essential quality is real, just like we know love is real. We know it when we feel it, and it is very real to us when we experience it.

Sensing Integrity

Once upon a time, the collective consciousness did not believe in the existence of germs, because science could not see or measure germs. Then the microscope was invented. Now germ theory is a fundamental tenet of medicine. This theory states that microorganisms, which are too small to be seen without the aid of a microscope, can invade the body and cause certain diseases. Until the acceptance of germ theory, diseases were often perceived as punishment for a person's evil behavior.[2]

What is invisible to the naked eye is not unreal. It is simply . . . invisible to the naked eye. So, too, is the invisible essence of integrity that expresses through coherent wave-based interference patterns. Organized movement. Organized flow. Organized glow.

Some of us see these waveforms with expanded perception, and we know they are every bit as real as coffee tables. Others hold hands with skepticism and wait for the tools to prove the existence of unseen realities.

Wherever we are on the continuum of knowing or doubting, trust that someday soon what is hidden will be revealed. Perhaps we will be able to calibrate integrity in the same way we may sit down for a cup of tea—with ease and grace.

Our settings for reality will change. The settings are changing now. Feel it. Know it. Trust it. Our hearts can calibrate integrity. Our hearts have an innate sensor for the Integrity Effect.

Integrity Is Our Business

Not everyone will do as he or she says and honor integrity through words, deeds, and actions. It is not up to us to ensure that others have integrity. That is a path of control.

It is only up to us to honor our own integrity, for this is the path of the heart. When we do as we say, and honor our words through deeds and actions, integrity honors us with the rippling of our True Authentic Magnificence.

Consider that anything that lacks integrity is not sustainable. The physics of integrity is enduring. And while it is our inherent birthright to honor our own integrity, it is not our responsibility for others to step into integrity. That is not our business.

It is our business to embody integrity and model it for others. We can help others map integrity simply by becoming it and expressing integrity from our hearts. We can hold space for others to step into integrity. We can hold space for everyone to become aware of the power and freedom of integrity. Awareness is power. Awareness is a key to opening the expansive doors of the Integrity Effect.

Integrity is a matter of choice. We are all free to choose integrity or not. We have free choice. However, choices made out of integrity are not free at all. There is a cost to not living in integrity that affects everyone.

There is a Ricochet Effect that occurs when we are not in integrity and when we are in relation to people or paradigms that are out of integrity. The Ricochet Effect will be explored later in this book, as it helps us map the gaps in the popular meme *"we create our own reality."*

Many are unaware of or do not comprehend the significance of the Integrity Effect. Some may think they can hide from themselves and hide from others in patterns of manipulation. Or they may pretend to be in integrity, which is still manipulation. Our hearts are hard-wired innately for authenticity as integrity and will recognize imposters. The physics of manipulation lacks congruity and, consequently, experiences will skew sideways. This might look like things totally falling apart when integrity altogether is not present.

Herein lies opportunity to step into integrity from our hearts. It is never too late. Integrity awaits us all, without judgment. Our hearts await us all without judgment.

Commitment to Integrity

When we make a heart-centered commitment to live in integrity, everything in our reality will begin to realign according to that resonance.

Patterns, situations, and circumstances as placeholders that do not match the congruence of integrity will become more pronounced. The contrast may intensify. We may be challenged with multiple opportunities to renew and strengthen our vow and commitment to integrity, our commitment to ourselves, and our commitment to something bigger than ourselves, yet still somehow us.

At times it will not be easy. But it will be worthwhile. For within heart-centered awareness and the Integrity Effect are all the key codes necessary to orchestrate extraordinary, joy-filled lives.

Integrity as Authenticity is love in action. Integrity is self-love. The effects of integrity ripple holonomically in all directions.

The Integrity Effect as Joy

The Integrity Effect closes the perceived gap between who we truly are (love as limitless potential) and how we have conditioned ourselves to be.

The Integrity Effect, characterized by authenticity and transparency, leads us to consistently access our joy no matter what appears to be happening. Joy is found in the connection to our authenticity, and joy occurs in the presence of the Integrity Effect. We tap into an inner volition of joy that is available to us even as we traverse challenging terrains. Joy is available to all of us, for joy is a natural side effect of heart-centered awareness.

As we move into the gap with integrity, we notice that the gap between where we are and where we want to be lessens. Moving into the gap also means no longer paying attention to how things need to change but connecting with the desired change as though it has already unfolded as an actualized experience. This connection bridges the gap such that the gap dissolves and evolves into a new experience of reality.

The Integrity Effect entails paying attention with intention to the truth of the wisdom of our hearts. We listen to our hearts and allow the mind to follow.

To move into the gap is to move into a space of grace as completion, an agape of love and compassion for self and others that only our hearts can truly reveal. The gap is filled by the eternal possibilities that allow for self-love, self-accountability, True Authentic Power, and True Authentic Relating to ripple into all that we create, manifest, and experience.

We move into the gap by realizing that the gap is at the heart of all sustained illusions and that the gap is no more real (or unreal) than our unmanifested desires. Never mind the gap. Move into the gap with integrity and notice that it is no longer there.

By approaching the gap from the eternal wisdom of our hearts, all is possible, and we become true Heartists effectively able to nurture True Authentic Desires, seeds of our inherent potential, into actual blossoming expressions of reality.

We move into the gap by living our joy, a form of elating and relating to the universe that comes not from the mind but from the endless well of limitless love that flows from within our hearts. We flow into abundance. We flow into the gap and notice through this movement that we already are what we desire to become.

By living from our hearts, we embrace integrity as a deep abiding connection to self and a deep abiding connection to the All that is. This integrity is not an individual I Experience but a collective We Experience, for integrity includes awareness of connection to everyone and everything.

Integrity Is Connection

Through the recognition of connection, we may consistently reconcile discrepancies within selves and our circumstances. Through heart-centered connections, we can bridge the gap between individual notions that we create our own reality and the external consensus of a shared reality that seems to happen beyond our perceived control.

We do create our own reality, and reality happens to us too. The two principles work together as one symbiotic, cohesive force, functioning in a perpetual feedback loop. We co-create in an interactive synergistic universe of unlimited potentials that is accessible in its entirety from the field of the heart.

A movement in awareness from the mind to the heart is moving into the gap with integrity. Our hearts serve as bridges to connect all gaps, distinctions, and expressions in that feedback loop. Through heart-centered connections, we may create and sustain structures that support us in return. We are able to move beyond rigid forms of external control to an inner dominion of freedom, flexibility, and flow. We move into limitless living.

Moving into the gap with integrity does not mean we dissolve all boundaries and parameters of our reality structures. Nor does it necessarily mean that individual and collective challenges instantly dissolve. Is it possible? Yes, anything is possible.

However, moving into the gap with integrity provides us with the ability to perceive value in distinctions as *placeholders* in awareness that serve as a catalyst for the power of choice.

Moving into the gap with integrity means accessing limitless potential and limitless choices. Limitless potential cannot be fathomed by the limiting nature of the mind. Move beyond the mind to the heart of completion, where there are no gaps. From the curious heart, we flow with ease and grace to a space where anything is really possible.

With openhearted curiosity, we make useful distinctions and may choose to live into the answer. The answer becomes . . . there is no gap. There is only love and limitless potential awaiting our recognition, connection, receivership, and expression.

Come join me as, together, we move into the gap, into the heart of integrity, to embrace shared new realities through love and limitless potential, leveraging a physics of love, heart–mind synthesis, and the power of choice.

Come discover the Joy of Being as we experience the Integrity Effect.

2

Everything Is You in Relation to ... Placeholders

We don't see things as they are, we see them as we are.

—Anais Nin

All that you experience is you in relation to—everything! Relating is a dynamic, ever-evolving essential of relationships. Relating describes you in relation to all. Relating is you in relation to—everything!

Everything is you in relation to . . . placeholders.

What is a placeholder?

I define a placeholder as any pattern of information in our resonant awareness that reflects back some aspect of *self-love as wholeness and completion* not yet recognized.

Placeholders literally and energetically hold places in our awareness. A placeholder may be anything in our reality to which we are relating in our lives. A placeholder may be a thought, emotion, problem, condition, mask, perceptual filter, or habituated behavior.

A placeholder may also be an opportunity, possibility, or potentiality not yet expressed. A placeholder may be a person, archetype, structure, or resonant field. Anything and everything in reality can be a placeholder for reflection.

All placeholders to which we are relating may be representations of self-love as reflective awareness or of the perceived absence of self-love.

As there is no external substitute for the inherent love that we are, all placeholders in our reality with which we resonate may serve as mirrors, shining back to us an aspect of ourselves we may not yet recognize, accept, integrate, transcend, or transform as part of our inherent wholeness.

Really, What Is Reality?

We can never truly know "reality." We can only know our experience of reality by virtue of how we perceive it. Our personal lens of awareness serves as a mechanism for noticing, perceiving, and experiencing reality. When we expand the apertures of our awareness, we are able to notice, perceive, and experience *more* of reality.

When we open our perceptions, we are able to experience more love as limitless potential. When we open our lens of awareness, we are able to project and reflect more love. When we open our hearts, we are able to connect to All as love and limitless potential.

Reference for Self-Love

For as long as I can remember, I have been fascinated with the reality creation process. I had hoped studying psychology in college would provide me with answers to the nature of reality, but academia and research only let me understand models for reality, not reality itself.

Models are maps for reality. Models can shape our understanding of reality, but they do not fully explain reality in relation to itself. Models also do not fully explain reality in relation to the individual or the collective. Models serve as placeholders for reality.

My roommate and best friend during senior year in college was someone I really appreciated. She was so . . . truly authentically herself, from the way she spoke to the choices she made to the way she would look at someone and know when he or she was telling the truth or a fib. She seemed to have a built-in bull-oney meter and wasn't afraid to use it to calibrate her experiences. In many respects, she was very intuitive, ever presently aware of herself and her surroundings, not in a self-conscious way but rather in a self-empowering way.

I suppose we were friends because we shared similar attributes and interests. We were both psychology majors; we loved the beach and volleyball, going to parties, and hanging out contemplating the meaning of life. We were in resonance. And yet what I admired most about her were her perceived differences from myself. In hindsight, I now recognize that these differences were not so different after all but were similar aspects of myself I had not yet embraced. What I saw in her was within me awaiting recognition: confidence, a unique style, an unapologetic approach to being wholly and truly herself, and a graceful manner of allowing these qualities to unfold as True Authentic Expression.

In comparison, I often felt like the ugly duckling, unaware of my grace, True Authentic Beauty (TAB), and individual way of swimming—navigating in my own special way, creating unique ripples in our shared reality pond. Inside, I didn't really like myself, and despite my academic and athletic accomplishments and popularity, I felt like an imposter. Surely it would be a matter of time before people figured out I wasn't worthy.

To this day, many years later, I still remember the gist of something she shared with me during one of our many conversations about life. *"I focus on relating, and everything organizes accordingly."*

There are certain times in our lives when words are spoken and, though we may not comprehend them intellectually, we somehow know them to be true. There is a knowing without knowing how we know. We may even find, despite the knowing, that we choose to reject or disagree with that perspective because it challenges our reference frames for reality.

At the time, I could not fully understand the significance of what she was saying, but the words really landed at home in my heart. I could not comprehend in my mind, possibly because I did not have a reference or language yet for what she was alluding to but did not actually say.

Now, I can look back fondly at my earlier self and see that I did know. On the surface, it seemed she was saying that she strives to get all her relationships right and then she is OK. But I knew her relationships were not always smooth and easy. As her roommate, I saw the challenges with her parents, sister, boyfriends, and professors. Yet she was always OK with herself, unwavering in her own being-ness, even amid the turmoil, and even when others were not OK with her. Her sense of who she was and her love for herself were not dependent on her relationships.

Several years later, I realized the magnitude of the gifts encoded within her words. And while we can never really know another person's experience, or exactly what he or she may say, in my interpretation, she was conveying, "I am complete as me in relation to me. And from that space of being complete with me I am able to connect as completion in relation to everything."

Although I did not yet have a reference for feeling complete within myself, I did have a reference for my friend, and so she (and her statement) became a powerful model in my awareness, something I would refer to again and again until I had mapped the experience for myself and no longer needed the model.

I began to wonder, then, as you might now, what would an experience of completion feel like? How could I be totally OK with me regardless of how others might perceive me? How might self-acceptance and self-love change the way I relate to myself?

How might self-love and authenticity change the way I relate to others and . . . how others relate to me? What thoughts, sensations, perceptions, or experiences might I notice? What if I could map this experience for myself and then embody it?

I remember initially trying to justify why I did not feel self-love and she did. I tried to compare and contrast our lives, as that is what our minds do. The mind compares and contrasts. I initially attributed her cohesive relationship to herself to her upbringing and family dynamics, economic affluence, good looks, and so on.

Yet, as much as I tried to account for why she loved herself and justify why I did not feel self-love, the more I realized the reasons didn't matter. What mattered was that I felt a genuine desire to experience self-love, for in that heart-filled desire was the seed of completion that was ready to grow.

Our heart's desires are seeds of love's completion ready to grow. We are seeds of love's completion ready to grow.

Placeholder for New References

Indeed, we are the meaning makers of reality. When how we relate to ourselves takes on new meaning, new connections and new experiences form, enabling the apertures of our awareness to expand. We establish new references as distinctions, and reality takes on new meaning too.

A beautiful facet of relating to our selves, situations, circumstances, challenges, opportunities, and desires from a framework of placeholders is that they do not hold the same meaning for us as they may have when they were problems, limitations, or conditions.

We are able to relate to them differently, and as a result, the placeholder no longer holds such an important place in our reality.

What Hooks Us Has Us

Another value of relating to everything in our reality through the context of placeholders is that we are more easily able to do so from a space of neutrality.

We are less likely to have a charge for or against a particular situation because placeholders enable our perceptual filters to lift, shift, expand, or release.

When the charge dissipates, we are neutral. When we are neutral, we are free.

Neutral does not mean we stop wanting what we want. Being neutral does not mean we stop wanting things to change. Instead, we are no longer hooked into whatever it is that we think needs to change. What hooks us has us. What hooks us keeps us tethered to the state of no change. When we have a charge for something needing to change, our filters will continue to observe no change. So we get more of the same. Being neutral as we relate to placeholders is what enables placeholders to transform to graceholders.

When we relate to something differently, how we experience reality changes. Perceiving our experiences of ourselves, and others, from the holo-frame of a placeholder enables us to encode new information beyond our habitual filters. Through placeholders, we are able to see beyond our perceptual filters and access an expanded state of love as awareness that is both self-empowering and transformational to our experience of reality.

From Placeholder to Graceholders

Graceholder is a term to describe the transformational process that occurs when we fully love ourselves such that the placeholder no longer holds the same value or power in our reality. As all placeholders represent some aspect of self-love or not loving self, when we bring self-love to the equation, a space of grace takes place. This is freedom and a facet of the Integrity Effect.

The process of transforming placeholders to graceholders can happen instantly or can occur over the continuum of time.

Recently, a student asked me if it is possible ever to transcend all placeholders into graceholders. My initial answer was yes, because anything is possible. My second answer was, *if that is the goal,* it is possible, but consider that the goal is not getting rid of placeholders altogether. In fact, there is no goal, as a goal implies an endpoint. Mapping self-love as authenticity and integrity is the only place-holder worth keeping, and those coordinates continue to evolve as we do.

What does tend to occur in the process of consistently interacting from the heart with placeholders is that the shift happens more and more quickly. The movement from charge to neutral becomes almost instantaneous. Often, nothing needs to happen other than to witness the pattern.

Then we are free to shift from neutral into accelerated gear moving forward. We may choose to focus on creating from completion, manifesting what we desire. Therein, again, we have placeholders that can represent opportunities: new projects, new potentials, probabilities and possibilities ready to actualize when we connect from the heart.

By virtue of relating to everything in the holo-frame of placeholders, many of our perceptual filters that serve as limitations can release, and we are able to map new trails for our reality based on love and limitless potential.

Love and Distinctions

As a young child at the age of five, I remember my mother sitting me down in the family room to share some important news: she and my father were getting a divorce. Because Dad was moving out of the house, taking his strong aversion to pets with him, we were told that my brother and I were going to get our much-desired puppy. I see now the humor of the exchange and possible bargaining chip: Dad for dog. Except that we had no choice. The choice was made for us.

I recall that on the day after receiving news of the divorce (D-day), we went dog shopping. My mom, brother, and I had gone to the local animal shelter to pick out our new dog. We looked at every dog in the shelter. Somewhat unrealistically, I wanted to take all of the doggies home. Nonetheless, we had fondly noticed a brother–sister puppy pair that we really were drawn to, but we could only have one dog. We all agreed it would be unfair to separate the two sibling pups from each other, so we did not choose them. Instead, we resigned to leaving the shelter empty-handed, disappointed, and without our new dog. We had let go of the idea as possibility, if only for the moment.

Literally as we were walking out the door of the animal shelter, we held the door open for a woman walking in. She was holding what appeared to me to be a giant cotton ball. Except this was a moving cotton ball! I soon realized she was cradling a three-week-old puppy in her arms.

The moment I laid eyes on that dog, it was as if time stood still, and the synchronicity of what I now consider "perfect universal timing" was evident. I somehow intuitively knew (a knowing without knowing how I knew) that that tiny white fluff ball was to be my puppy. He was white like salt, and yet I also knew his name would be Pepper. The irony of a white dog being called Pepper (a black seasoning) would later strike me as quite humorous, as nothing is ever truly black or white. Everything has shades of grays (as grace).

Pepper was my saving grace, a powerful placeholder for love. It seems I had projected all my love and emotions surrounding my recently shattered family into his awesome puppiness. In turn, he reflected back to me the experience of unconditional love, perhaps a gift from a universe that wanted me to stay curious, vulnerable, and open. In the presence of Pepper, my heart was full of delight. Our connection was love, a connection that sustained me during a very difficult period of childhood.

As is perhaps common for many young children of divorce, I felt the divorce was my fault. If only I had been a better child, with fewer needs, perhaps Mommy and Daddy would have stayed together. I thought I had created the reality of the divorce. This thought and associated emotions created an imprint for a map of coordinates I would carry with me (consciously and unconsciously) for many years to come, influencing many life choices.

Yet coupled with the experience of a painful divorce was simultaneous sheer delight in the manifestation of a little white bundle of fluffy joy, my puppy dog Pepper. He was my new best friend, and he was pure love in my experience.

After the divorce, I actually remember wondering if reality happened to me, or if I create my reality. This was perhaps an odd question for a young child. But pain can evoke a depth of curiosity and wisdom far beyond our chronological years.

To me, at the time, it did not seem logical that the things I did not want (such as my parents divorcing each other) just happened to me, but the things I did want (like a puppy) were of my own creation.

Either I created the circumstances, or the circumstances happened to me. Did reality just happen? Maybe sometimes we were lucky? I wondered then (as I still ponder now) what our individual role is in creating reality. Why is it that sometimes we get what we want and other times we get pummeled with a series of events and experiences that feel nothing like puppy love? What about other people's roles in creating our individual reality, other people's choices, and what of our mutual roles in creating shared reality?

Life continued rather differently following the divorce, as both parents remarried within a year to new spouses, each with children of his or her own. A judge granted my mother sole custody of me, while my brother went to live with my father. (In hindsight, I see irony in not wanting to separate the brother–sister puppies at the animal shelter— an interesting foreshadowing of future events.)

My time with my parents, brother, and new stepsiblings was divided, and soon there were divided loyalties, and divided possessions too. It seemed to me that everything in my life reflected division . . . except Pepper. He was a placeholder for unconditional love to me, and he comforted my broken heart in ways my mind could not understand.

Is Any of This Absolutely True?

Perhaps none of this is the way it really happened, and perhaps none of this is absolutely true. Maybe it is only relatively true to me, based on how I interpreted the experiences, based on my perceptual filters. However, as Anais Nin so astutely noted, we never really see things as they truly are. We see things as we are.

As a young child who felt somehow responsible for her family becoming a house divided, this core perception stood as a foundational reality construct, a template or map that shaped how I perceived myself and all that I related to in my life.

This reality construct served as a powerful filter for perceiving many more experiences of similar resonance, further defining and reinforcing my sense of separation, divisiveness, and lack of self-love. As a teenager and young adult, I developed strategies to avoid myself or to compensate for this lack of self-love, including repetitive illness, eating disorders, addictions, and cycles of under/overachievement.

Do I blame the divorce? No. There is no blame. Many children go through divorces and still love themselves. Yet there is value in recognizing how our experiences create filters for our reality that then serve as maps for future life paths. The pattern of the divorce was mapped into my awareness, and regardless of whether I created that reality (or it simply happened to me), it still happened. The experience created filters for my projector; filters for my lens of awareness. This was in turn *reflected* in how I related to myself, and to others. In this *projection* and *reflection,* I made the *connection* that I was not OK. My skewed perceptions led to guilt, shame, blame, sorrow, and insecurity—about myself and in relation to the world at large.

Yet, almost miraculously, amid this separation and self-condemnation, the universe delivered a beautiful puppy dog that also served as a pivotal placeholder in my life. Pepper became my reference for unconditional love, delight, joy, and wonder. In this projection and reflection of pure puppy love, I made a connection to All that is love too. Amid the limitation, fear, and division I was experiencing, there was also a presence and awareness of unity, love, and joy. Reality for me was love and *distinctions,* expressions that appeared to be anything other than love.

Innocence/Inner Sense

Perhaps you have had pivotal moments or circumstances in your life that may have heralded the end of innocent perception and childlike wonder? This perceived ending was brought forth by events that shifted you out of resonance with a loving universe of limitless possibility, trust, wonder, and delight into a reality seemingly filled with limitation, separation, and/or fear of what dread may come.

Perhaps you can relate to a loss of innocence (an inner sense of love) based on your own experiences? Perhaps powerful placeholders, holo-framed imprints from the past, still out-picture for you today, as though the old maps are still being followed with continued resonance?

What we may not realize is that our limiting experiences do not define us. We are still love as unbounded potential, even if we may closely identify with the various circumstances we encountered that felt like anything other than love. We are still love as limitless potential, even when we have experiences that look and feel like limitations.

Integration: True Authentic Self (TAS)

What if you were able to consistently access and embody limitless potential, unconditional love, and joy no matter what may have happened, or what seems to be happening now? What if it is entirely possible, and practical, to embrace and integrate your true essence (as unconditional love and limitless potential) with your self-contained perceived limitations—all your placeholders?

Consider what it would be like to live peacefully and harmoniously in an undivided house of consciousness, filled with many rooms of self-love and self-appreciation? What if your placeholders could evolve into graceholders?

What if you could live, relate, and elate through the Integrity Effect?

The embodiment of True Authentic Self (TAS), a being of unconditional love and limitless potential, having experiences that feel and seem like limitations, is a gateway to extraordinary, empowered, joy-filled lives.

Embodying True Authentic Self is an important component of the Integrity Effect. Living as True Authentic Self is not about being perfect; it is about being perfectly imperfect, including all the aspects of ourselves that we may want to change. As TAS, our perfect limitless nature eternally dances alongside our finite limitations or deemed imperfections.

Limitless potential as unconditional love is who we are in our core essence. Our core essence, our True Self, is always available through the field of the heart.

Conversely, our Authentic Self is the experience of limitation and confusion as well as all the notions and emotions that may accompany this confusion. These mapped patterns are simply placeholders for how we may perceive ourselves. They are our perceptual filters. Perceptual filters are the lenses we look through to make sense of our reality.

Our Authentic Self is essentially who we think we are, based on how we have defined ourselves from our limited experiences. Although the limitations may not necessarily be true, when we resonate with them as if they *are* true, then our reality will conform accordingly.

The perceptions we hold, whether they are beliefs, thoughts, or feelings, serve as the filters through which we experience reality. Everything is experienced through our filters. This is our reality bubble, which is often clouded with confusion. Clear the filters and reality will take on a whole new brilliance. We embrace our whole brilliance.

The synthesis of True Self as abundant love–limitless potential, combined with our Authentic Self, that which experiences limitation, is the liberating experience of living and loving our True Authentic Self. As TAS, we are both limitless potential and limitation united peacefully together as one, in the same way we create our reality *and* *reality* happens to us.

The True Self component of TAS is the All that *is* creating our reality from unlimited potential and infinite creative intelligence. True Self is the self of miracles, magic, and synchronistic puppy dog manifestations. The True Self is essentially impersonal consciousness potential or perfect and complete unconditional love. Our True Self is connected to All as One, divine and sustainable, without personal qualifiers or identifiers.

The Authentic Self component of TAS is the part of the self that responds to reality with its plethora of placeholders. Authentic Self includes our self-contained perceived limitations, including the habitual programs we may run that tell us we are anything other than . . . boundless love. The Authentic Self is the finite part of our being possibly perceived as being fundamentally flawed, inherently lacking, and imperfect. The Authentic Self is the self as individual, separate, and differentiated. Authentic Self is "only human."

Unity of Limitlessness with Limitation

Integration of the True Self (limitless potential and unconditional love) with the Authentic Self (limitations and conditions) allows for an acceptance of all parts of our being to cohesively exist together as one. Acceptance. Authenticity. Integrity.

As a result, we are able to serve up our own reality and respond to what reality may be returning to us in the most empowering of manners.

Reality is a little bit like playing tennis. Our True Self serves up the ball to the universe to instigate the game. The universe may return the ball, often with unexpected speed, curve, and force. Sometimes the ball will come out of nowhere in a way that seems completely unrelated to our serve, both in time and space. Sometimes multiple balls are returned simultaneously. However, all is connected. How we respond to those balls varies to the degree we may have integrated and embodied True Authentic Self (TAS).

In truth, limitations are not really limitations at all; rather, they are expressions of limitless potential in a finite parameter, a boundary of which is still inherently connected to limitless potential. Limitations are placeholders still connected to our core essence as unconditional love and unbounded potential.

As we will learn throughout this book, limitations are not necessarily hindrances. When integrated, limitations can serve as springboards to magnificence in the interactive reality creation process.

Rather than limitations being something we need to release, transform, or transcend, limitations can serve as powerful placeholders in our awareness, effectively changing the way we relate to . . . everything.

Reality is up for grabs, and sometimes our hands are fully occupied with responding to the balls that are being served in our direction. When we live from the field of the heart as our TAS, we will be empowered to create and relate to anything. When we change the way we relate to ourselves, we change the way everything relates to us.

Heart Has No Gaps

Living as our True Authentic Self from the field of the heart is how we playfully move into the gap to discover the

Integrity Effect, our inherent power and genuine capacity for extraordinary living.

As a result of embodying TAS, we are able to experience self-love and authenticity, and we may thrive cohesively as individuals within the collective community of shared reality. We get to be fully and wholly who we truly are, living our unique signature, however it may occur for us.

The field of the heart is a gateway to True Authentic Self and the Integrity Effect.

The field of the heart is the nexus for truth as unity.

The field of the heart is a portal to All as love. All as love and distinctions. All as love and placeholders. All as one expressing through individuality. All as you and me in relation to . . . the WE experience.

As we shall soon discover, the field of the heart is our innate GPS for navigating through all terrains of consciousness. We have the ability to create new maps for ourselves based on love and limitless potential.

When we play from the field of the heart, we serve reality from an inner volition of love as completion. We are empowered to PLAY it forward.

Let's PLAY it forward.

3

Mapping Unity

It was the best of times, it was the worst
of times, it was the age of wisdom, it was
the age of foolishness, it was the epoch
of belief, it was the epoch of incredulity,
it was the season of Light, it was the
season of Darkness, it was the spring of
hope, it was the winter of despair, we had
everything before us,
we had nothing before us.

—Charles Dickens, *A Tale of Two Cities*

These words, written by Charles Dickens in 1859, could easily apply to many aspects of modern-day life. It is both the best of times and worst of times, depending on our perspective, depending on our resonance, and depending on how we choose to relate to what appears to be happening.

How we choose to relate to what is happening in all facets of our lives influences our ability to integrate, transform, and transcend all perceived conditions and circumstances.

Unknown Coordinates

Consider that humanity is in a position that we have never been previously. We are in new and entirely unfamiliar terrain. As Dickens wrote, "we [have] everything before us, we [have] nothing before us."

From a strictly horizontal perspective, if we look at what seems to be occurring, we might conclude that the world is falling apart. It is the worst of times. Our environments seem toxic, our governments are in flux, our economies are threatened, and traditional prevailing paradigms are under scrutiny, revealing deception and breeding distrust. Fear is rampant.

Wherever we turn, there seems to be a breaking down of the structures and systems that have largely driven our experience of order in everyday reality. There is chaos. Collective reality is in flux.

However, when we look at what "appears" to be happening from an expanded frame of reference, through heart-centered awareness, we also gain a vertical perspective that essentially gives us an eternal, albeit synchronized, view; we can see that things are not necessarily falling apart. Rather, they are coming together in an entirely new way.

A vertical perspective enables us to see that the horizontal paths we have been traveling are limiting and may not be sustainable; rather, they may serve only to perpetuate destruction, distraction, and disconnection for the individual and collective WE experience.

Old paradigms based on fear, division, and control are reconfiguring. These old structures are dissolving so we may evolve into new realities based on unity, love, connection, integration, and individual command as an extension of community.

We are indeed at a crossroads where following old maps and old ways of doing things will not lead us to sustainability. As long as we follow old maps, we will continually re-encode for more of the same. Our past will always catch up to us because we are continually re-creating old programs based on outmoded imprints we continue to follow. Old maps will not navigate us through the morphing terrain.

This crossroads is where the heart of it all intersects with the power of choice.

What new maps will we create? How will we choose to PLAY?

Mapping Trust

Recently I was scheduled to speak at a local weekend conference fewer than sixty miles from my home. I had planned to drive to the conference in the mornings and return home in the evenings. I looked forward to the leisurely drive as a time to reflect, while my trusted GPS in my car would seamlessly navigate me from point A (my home) to point B (the conference location) and back home at night.

While still in my driveway, I programmed the GPS with the address coordinates of my intended destination, the conference. As I backed out of the driveway in reverse to move forward on the street, I was ready to enjoy the ride. I loved driving in my old convertible car that I purchased when I resigned from the pharmaceutical industry. It was an important placeholder in my reality, symbolizing freedom from years of mandated company vehicles and, more importantly, emancipation from a career in drugs for Corporate America.

My freedom car, while not new, was dearly appreciated as a fun way to cruise to wherever I needed to go. To help make driving easy, particularly in new cities, I had a high-technology GPS installed a few years after buying the car. However, my new career teaching consciousness-expanding seminars required frequent travel by plane, so the GPS and the car often sat idle for weeks at a time.

Between my older trusted vehicle and the seldom used fancy navigation system, I was certain I would arrive at my expected destination on time without getting lost. During the course of the driving journey, there were a few unexpected redirects, even though I had been following the directions meticulously. About forty minutes into the commute, I began to suspect something was off. The system kept making recalculations to my route. According to the original estimations, I should have arrived at my destination already. I was getting concerned. Yet, I continued to trust the map and followed the navigation system, which surely had more information than me.

Or so I thought, because just as I was beginning to worry, the GPS proudly exclaimed, "Arriving at destination." However, my arrival point was a 7–11 convenience store on a dead-end street. This was not the location of my conference. In fact, as I looked more closely at the address that my GPS had rerouted me to, I realized I was not even in the same city as the conference.

Somehow my GPS had gone awry. Or did it? It was at that moment that I realized my GPS software had not been updated for eight years. I was following old maps. My car was navigating a map of geographical terrain that was in existence many years ago. Not now. The roads and highways had literally been rebuilt. New roads were created, old roads closed, new structures erected, and the maps we historically followed years ago no longer matched the existing territory. The landscape had changed.

How often do we follow old maps and expect them to get us to our desired destination when the terrain has transformed or morphed into something different?

Moreover, how often do we look outside ourselves to other people or surrogate power structures for guidance on where to go, what to do, rather than trusting ourselves? Although there is nothing wrong with asking for help or directions, when doing so becomes a default strategy, it may be a form of self-avoidance and lack of self-trust.

This experience of the GPS system gone awry triggered a fond memory of a three-week road trip with my partner through Costa Rica several years ago. We had been forewarned by seasoned travelers and locals alike not to follow the printed road maps that were available everywhere. We were advised not to trust the maps because they were obsolete. Torrential rains and mudslides often wiped out the roads and highways. The maps were seldom updated, as it was almost impossible to keep up with the changing terrain. Thus the maps ultimately led unsuspecting visitors awry.

Despite the warnings, we drove three hours toward a major national monument according to a published map, only to end up in a local family's backyard, where they were washing laundry in an adjacent stream.

Initially I was perturbed we had wasted so much time driving, following wrong directions to a road that only led us to soggy pajamas. However, there was such humor, surprise, and delight in the encounter of the family laundering together that we were left with a sense to just let go and enjoy the ride.

We let go. Therein was an invitation to choose to trust our hearts and follow intuitive inspiration.

We threw out our maps. The remainder of our trip was devoid of maps and filled with unexpected synchronicity. Once we stopped following the obsolete versions of the terrain, our journey became one of the best trips ever, filled with flow, joy, surprise, and delight. We immersed ourselves in the culture and truly experienced the country's mantra, "*Pura vida,*" meaning "Pure life."

Consider that the pure life is recognizing that it is truly OK when things do not work out as expected. Things always work out. It's our expectations that don't always work. Trust.

Trust the heart. It always knows.

Heart-Field as GPS

The field of the heart contains an inner navigation system, a GPS pointing the way to our own true north while always mapping us in love's direction. This GPS system, while eternal, calibrates coordinates based on the truth of unity and limitless potential in real time. Now. Always. The GPS of the heart can be trusted.

The unlimited field of the heart always knows what the limited mind may have forgotten. Living and experiencing from the field of the heart is easy, once we stop living and experiencing any other way.

As the field of the heart does not take things apart, the experience of being in the field of the heart can be very unifying. We may experience ourselves as completion. We may experience ourselves as our true essence of love, void of programming. We may experience self-acceptance and authenticity.

Consistently living from the field of the heart enables us to be our True Authentic Self living the Integrity Effect. Inside our hearts are new maps for navigating new terrains from a space of completion.

Language of Light

Through the language throughout the pages of this book are a plethora of access points for creating and relating to self, others, and reality from heart-centered awareness, a space of love as inclusion.

This is a new language enabling us to map a truth of unity as completion from within, as we relate to . . . everything. This language supports us in connecting to what is innate to everyone and, in so doing, opens us to a plethora of possibilities.

This language helps us access the voluminous potential inherent to our hearts through embodied experiences while assisting us to navigate more proficiently through life's challenges. The language can quench a thirst for self-love and connection, enabling us to flow more freely into the recognition of our own True Authentic Magnificence.

Water Flows Open

I have always been fascinated with the life story of Helen Keller, who was both blind and deaf and yet led an extraordinarily accomplished existence. I admired her triumph over perceived limitations driven by an incessant desire to connect. When Helen Keller first grasped the idea that a word spelled into her hand corresponded to the water flowing over her hand, it was a huge epiphany.

It was an *ah-ha* moment.

This insight alone led her to make connections and open doors of knowledge, opportunity, and experiences previously closed to her. Once Helen grasped the new language of signs as symbols to describe what she was experiencing, this enabled her (and many others) to see, speak, and communicate with a world that was previously inaccessible. She connected from a void of darkness through a language that brought the unseen realities to light.

Many students have shared with me that through the unique language articulated through my teachings and writings about heart-centered awareness, placeholders, and TAS, they have many ah-ha moments. Furthermore, some have shared that they finally have a whole system for mapping what they have always known to be true for them but did not know quite how to describe, access, connect to, or implement.

Perhaps more importantly, they now have a flexible structure to support them in relating to . . . everything. You now have a flexible structure to support you in creating and relating to . . . everything.

Within the pages of this book are also a plethora of tools for accessing our own innate GPS through the field of the heart, coupled with the power of the mind so we may effectively create and choose to follow new maps, leading to new trails for our reality. We all have the power to create new imprints for reality. This power rests within our hearts. The power is the Integrity Effect.

Simply because things have always been a certain way does not mean that's the way things are or will always be. We have the opportunity to transcend the imprints and maps encoded in the past to bring forth new, expanded templates based on love, abundance, unity, and limitless potential.

Intuitive Logic

We all have an inner knowing, a knowing without knowing how we know—our intuition. This intuition guides us forward with both vertical and horizontal awareness. Heart-centered awareness gives us vertical and horizontal awareness, providing us with the ability to see the whole picture, beyond the surface of horizontal happenings.

Heart-centered awareness gives us 360-degree vision from multiple angles of awareness simultaneously.

Intuition is logic for the Heart. Through the field of the heart, we can innately intuit and create new blueprints effective for navigating through any terrain of consciousness now, to create changes for ourselves and for humanity moving forward.

Intuition, a facet of heart-centered awareness, is actually normal functioning, but many have left this resource dormant based on conditioning and perceptual filters. Off with the filters and into the heart as we access our TAS and the Integrity Effect!

We are all intuitive. We all have access to a unified field of interconnected information through our hearts. If we allow ourselves to expand the apertures of our awareness into realizing that being intuitive is as easy as breathing, as easy as eating, that intuition is a natural part of who we are, then creating new maps from the heart can become like a stroll at the beach.

Heart-Prints

Consider reality creation to be like a barefoot stroll on the beach with expansive sand dunes. Notice that there are many different footprints in the sand: in front of us, behind us, next to us, imprints everywhere created in myriad directions. If we follow the prints linearly, we can map a path that is clearly laid out in front of us.

Perhaps in the past we may have chosen to follow specific sets of footprints, maps created by others, paths that promised to take us to our desired destinations. At times those paths seemed comfortable, even to our unique footprints. Occasionally, new paths may have felt a little bigger than our footprints, but we acclimated and followed the map anyway. We grew into the imprints. All the while, the steps guided us in progression toward the expression of our own authenticity and integrity.

Eventually we may have outgrown the maps of the paths that were created by others. As the tides and currents change the shoreline of our own reality, and we change too, we may notice the incongruence between our hearts and the paths we are on. Thus, we may choose to step into something new or different. Or we may ignore the misgivings of our trusted heart connection by choosing to continue on the paths that we no longer feel aligned with. Either way, whether we follow the old familiar paths or follow our hearts to make a change, we will make useful distinctions. We are free to choose.

We are free to choose to trust our hearts and to step into fresh sands that bear no prints, creating new heart-prints. All the while, we create new maps, we respect those that have gone before us, those who walk next to us, and those who may choose to follow us. We are reminded to trust in ourselves and to remember, just like those who walked before us, that we have all the resources necessary to create new maps for extraordinary living now. We will know what to do, as the path of the heart is a path of wisdom.

We are reminded that no path is superior or inferior to any other map. All are simply different. Different is different. All paths, with their varying footprints, are sole/soul imprints of the all. When we choose to follow the path of the heart, with integrity, we honor all paths, even if we do not agree with all choices.

Integrity honors all. Integrity also honors that others' choices may not be right for us and so we are free to step away. We leverage choice with discernment. We are free to choose anew. We are free to make heart-prints in whatever direction our joy may flow.

We may not know where we are going to go in the very next moment, but we can allow for the field of the heart, our inner GPS, to guide us. When we trust our hearts and honor our unique soul signatures, we experience the Joy of Being. We experience the Integrity Effect.

The journey of heart-centered awareness does not necessarily occur in a linear fashion, like mentally plotting coordinates on a map; rather, the journey of the heart mapping process is holo-fractal, just like our heart-fields.

Fractal means that the same basic pattern is repeated on all scales. *Holo-* means that the whole is represented within all points within a certain system. This means that all of the coordinates we map from our hearts, the various ways of relating from our hearts, always occur from a space of wholeness and completion.

Heart-centered awareness is wholeness and completion. Love is wholeness and completion. Love is what we are, even if our awareness has migrated far away from this recognition.

The journey of heart-centered awareness is a journey of inclusion where we see the all in small and the small in all. We are able to notice seeds of love's completion in absolutely everything, even that which appears to be anything other than love.

Multiple Points on the Map

Heart-centered awareness gives us the ability to occupy multiple perspectives simultaneously. When we are able to look at reality, our lives (and the lives of others) from multiple perspectives, including various points of view, including multiple maps, separate neurosis evolves into symbiosis.

Acceptance and compassion for self and others may be found in freeing ourselves from any fixed map or point of view. How many points of view can we occupy simultaneously? The many is infinite . . . as all points stem from that which is pointless and limitless, including all points as part of the whole.

We may be at an unknown location for humanity, or at an intersection in our own lives where we are aware that the old is no longer working. We may not be sure how to proceed. We may wander while we wonder what new will look like, and what new really means. Despite the uncertainty, we do know what new means. Our hearts know. Our hearts always know. We can choose to trust our hearts.

Inside our hearts, our inner chambers of unbounded potential, are all the coordinates we need to navigate these changing times, maps of completion moving forward, in delight. We shall trust the inner mappings of our hearts, as we find contentment in the contents that pour forth from this limitless resource.

Come PLAY. Our heart-fields await us!

4

Becoming True Heartists
In-Joy

*The best and most beautiful things in the
world cannot be seen nor touched but are
felt in the heart.*

—Helen Keller

Perhaps you can think of a situation or a series of events when you just knew something without knowing how you knew. You may have experienced this feeling or inclination without any factual evidence to support what you were sensing. Soon you learned that what you were tracking was correct. Maybe you allowed your logical mind to convince you otherwise, only later to have kicked yourself for being remiss?

Had you trusted this hunch, paying attention to the cues, you would have been following your heart. Some call this intuition. Others call this gut instinct. I call it heart-centered awareness.

For centuries, the adage of "follow your heart" has been passed along through multiple generations across cultures. Many instinctively know that the heart can be trusted.

The heart has historically been linked to traits such as compassion, forgiveness, empathy, appreciation, and kind-ness. In the fourth century B.C., the Greek philosopher

Aristotle identified the heart as the seat of intelligence, motion, and sensation. In the late twelfth century, Master Nicolaus of Salerno declared that the physical heart was the primary "spiritual member" of the body. As such, the heart was considered the seat of all emotions.[1]

Yet in the postindustrial, modern technology–driven Information Age (Computer/Digital Age), the mind has taken the lead and the heart has been largely left behind. Western society has programmed the individual to focus on knowledge, data collection, and intellectual pursuits as though the mind/body is like a computer hard drive.

Well, if the mind/body is like a computer, then the heart-field is the connection to the universal Internet, with access to limitless information, love, creativity, inspiration, and innate boundless potential.

Why Heart-Centered Awareness?

The field of the heart is a gateway to a consciousness of completion. The heart does not take things apart. The heart, like love, has no polarity or opposite. Living from the unified heart rather than from the polarized mind enables us to move beyond limiting gaps in awareness to a limitless space of possibilities.

The intelligence of the heart connects us to the whole picture and attunes us to our innate intuition channel. Heart-centered awareness enables us to transcend the perceptual filters of the mind and reactive emotions based on those filters so we can relate to ourselves, and others, from a space of self-love as completion. Heart-centered awareness fully fills all gaps with love as unbounded potential. All expressions created from the heart, as truth in unity, will project and reflect love's completion accordingly.

What Is the Heart-Field?

There are many definitions of the heart-field that various individuals and organizations may utilize to talk about living from the heart. The heart-field I am referring to is not the physical heart, the heart-chakra, nor even the electromagnetic field of the heart that can be measured by certain devices.

However, the heart-field I am referring to includes the physical heart, the heart-chakra, as well as the electromagnetic field of the heart, for the heart-field is all-inclusive. The heart-field includes everything.

The field of the heart provides us with direct access to our inner voice, our inner wisdom, and our inner realm of limitless potential. The field of the heart creates a direct connection with our core essence, the true me and you.

The heart-field enables us to embody a coherent state of awareness, thus bypassing the segregation and limitations of the mind to access the totality of ourselves. In the heart-field, we tap into our innate potential by connecting to the most genuine part of ourselves, which knows itself as whole, limitless, and even timeless.

The field of the heart is a tube torus comprising two torsion fields. Torsion fields are spiraling antennae that send and receive information to and from the body as well as to and from the environment. Torsion field physics explains how our intuition works. There is a lot of scientific information to support this assertion, and I have written of torsion field science extensively in other books.

The torsion fields of the heart-field resemble a doughnut comprising two counterrotating fields, with the inner torsion field spinning in one direction and the outer torsion field spinning in the opposite direction. Within these torsion fields, there is a vortex or a still point. Within the vortex, information as potential couples with both of the enfolding torsion fields. This creates a certain amount of inertia and momentum simultaneously, which helps the information pop through this vacuum as form, action, and experience. Information (inform-in-action) as possibility creates experience directly from the field of the heart. When we access the field of the heart, we access pure potentiality *prior to* that potentiality expressing as form and experience.

One reason we drop down into the field of the heart is because it allows us to access a state of pure potentiality and neutrality. From the field of the heart, we can access undifferentiated states of information and consciousness potential *before* the information separates into form and defines itself through action, perspective, and/or experience.

According to research conducted at HeartMath Institute, the heart generates the body's most powerful and most extensive rhythmic electromagnetic field. Compared to the electromagnetic field produced by the brain, the electrical component of the heart's field is about sixty times greater in amplitude and permeates every cell in the body. The magnetic component is approximately five thousand times stronger than the brain's magnetic field and can be detected several feet away from the body with sensitive magnetometers.[2]

The heart-field is presumed to spin in two directions at the same time, clockwise and counterclockwise. As I have been shown through my own intuitive guidance, the torsion field spinning to the left is associated with access to our innate limitless potential, infinite information, and intuition, while the torsion field spinning to the right is associated with action, manifestation, expression, and choice.

We require both left-handed spin and right-handed spin together to function cohesively. Left is not better than right, and right is not better than left. Both are necessary, albeit different.

Left-handed spin and right-handed spin are simply a matter of perspective. Imagine you are standing facing me. Your left would be my right, and vice versa. So direction of spin depends on vantage point.

A more accurate description of heart-field spin would be that as one spiral spins inwardly, the other spiral spins outwardly. There is an ongoing involution and evolution that occur simultaneously. Where the two merge is a nexus point for infinite potential to express as distinction and experience.

The heart-field is our connection to everything, including our intuition. The field of the heart is where our personal sense of individual self meets transpersonal awareness in that we connect to something bigger than ourselves that is still somehow us. The heart-field is a portal into the soul and is an open source for truth. The heart-field is a trustworthy resource for getting reliable information. The heart-field functions like antennae receiving information from our own personal intuition channel. Through our hearts, we can access knowing without knowing how we know.

> *I've been questing most of my adult life for a deeper sense of self, a deeper meaning to explain away the horrific experiences of childhood and a deeper understanding of me in connection to all of life. I've studied many techniques with many "masters" of their various modalities. Melissa Joy crossed my path in 2011 and altered it in exponential ways that continue to unfold, surprise, inspire, and transform. Perhaps the most powerful gift I've gleaned from Melissa through her teachings and her "being-ness" is to give up the quest! She advocates deepening your connection to heart-centered awareness as your source to all you've been seeking outside yourself. Melissa embodies the concept in actualization of remembering from wholeness rather than seeking from the space of "not enough." Adding the simple question to my daily experiences of "Am I seeking or remembering?" has been a game-changer in bolstering my intuitive knowingness, creating space for True Authentic Relating with self and others, while allowing flow and grace in even the most difficult situations.* —KO

Sometimes people assume that they are not in their hearts when they are using their logical minds, as though the two are mutually exclusive. It has been my experience that this is not true. In fact, often people *are* in their hearts and something will seem so right and make so much sense that they assume logic is leading the way. However, intuition is logic for the Heart. Often our hearts will speak to us very pragmatically.

Consider that we do not need to reside in our hearts at the exclusion of our minds. In the next chapter, we will discuss how to leverage both heart and mind, what I refer to as *heart–mind synthesis*. For now, let's consider how we can become more aware of being in our hearts or *not* being in our hearts, so we can cultivate more heart-centered awareness.

How Do We Truly Know?

One of the most common questions I receive from students all around the world is, How do I truly know I am in my heart? This is a beautiful question that many inquiring minds want to know and perhaps only the heart can genuinely answer.

A fallacy that tends to occur for people wanting to experience being in the heart is *thinking* that there is any particular right or wrong way to access heart-centered awareness. Consider that there are as many different ways to experience being in our hearts as there are unique individuals on the planet. There is no right or wrong way to experience heart-centered awareness. Right or wrong is a concept of the mind that attempts to polarize and judge all experience.

In the same way we can never really know reality—we can only know our experience of reality—we can never really know definitively that we are in our hearts. We can only know our own experience of being in the heart. This experience of heart-centered awareness is unique to everyone. Thus it is important that we trust what we notice and experience when mapping awareness to our own heart-field. Trust what you experience.

Consider that, in a sense, we are always in our hearts. The heart-field is integral to our being. Our heart-field is connected to our core essence. Thus we are always in our hearts, as our core essence never changes and never goes anywhere. It is not possible not to be in our hearts, as the heart-field is what we are. However, it is very possible to move our awareness away from the *recognition* of heart-centered awareness.

How might this occur? Perhaps we have developed a persona or identity that we believe requires us always to be logical. Our career may depend on the reliance on our minds to perform linear tasks with a great degree of precision. Maybe we have learned that the best way to accomplish things in life is to predominantly use our minds.

It is possible that we may have learned at a very young age that being in our hearts was not a safe space. Perhaps we lost someone we loved when we were young and the pain was unbearable. Maybe we weren't nurtured or loved by our parents, and we encoded at a very young age that the universe is not a safe place. So we developed strategies for navigating through our lives logically to perceive ourselves as being one step ahead of what might get us.

As tiny children, we are almost always in our hearts, open and receptive to the world, brimming with childlike wonder. But maybe in our innocence, when we were in our hearts, someone hurt our feelings or ridiculed us so badly that we shut down our own access to our heart to protect the most cherished part of ourselves, our essence of wholeness as completion. So we built up an energetic wall around our hearts and then developed keen intellectual skills to overcompensate.

Or maybe we developed a strategy where our consciousness wasn't even inside our bodies and we sort of checked out. We decided not to be fully present so we could avoid being hurt again. We were not at home in our bodies because we were not at home in our hearts.

Perhaps we are filled with fear, and so we spend a significant amount of time ruminating about the past or anxiously anticipating the future. This habit takes our awareness out of the heart of now and the gifts that heart-centered presence has to offer.

For some, we are supersensitive or have even been labeled as empathic, and the only way we know how to cope with "feeling other people's stuff" is by staying disconnected from what we feel. We reside in the mind to protect ourselves from feeling anything. Perhaps we are unaware that we are all empathic and highly sensitive but some people are just more in tune to this sense than others. Empathy and sensitivity, forms of compassion, are facets of the human experience and the fact that we are all connected.

All the aforementioned can result in moving our awareness away from being present to our heart-fields. Regardless of the reasons, no matter how far our awareness has migrated from the field of the heart, no matter how long we have been away from our hearts, we can always find our way home.

Anywhere and Here

The *idea* of being in our hearts (or not) is a construct that can either constrict us or assist us. When leveraged properly, this construct enables us to build extraordinary experiences for ourselves and others. To me, our heart-field is a portal into an expanded knowingness that goes beyond the confines of the conscious mind. The heart knows. The heart itself is clairvoyant. The heart is able to see clearly. The term *clairvoyance* (from French *clair,* meaning "clear," and *voyance,* meaning "vision") means "clear seeing." In a sense, clear seeing never really occurs from our interpretive minds, as we always see through our perceptual filters. However, the heart connects to all information before the mind lens assumes its view.

The heart is like the ripples in a giant pond of water. If we were to observe the ripples from the heart, we would describe them as a meaningless swirl of interference patterns. However, the mind can observe the ripples and choose a focal point to interpret. We might all observe the same ripples in the pond, but our mental filters will generate different perceptions. This often happens in car accidents when eyewitness testimonials vary significantly based on the observers' unique angles and distinct memory recall.[3]

> *Heart-Centered Awareness and being authentically you! So beautiful! Resonance with yourself. Quiet joyfulness. Let your awareness sit here and then act. So easy. Simply You! This is very different from asking yourself "what would I do if I were to act from my heart?" asking the mind to come up with this answer. So many of us do this. We TRY to DO the heart-centered thing rather than simply becoming heart-centered and acting. From heart-centered awareness, there is a simple movement toward thought and action that does not originate in the mind. It originates from the knowing that is purely there in your heart space.*
>
> *It seems very vague, but experienced, it is very concrete and real.*
>
> *Melissa radiates this truth. Reading or listening to her books, being with her at a seminar, or engaging her in dialogue—all lead to the deep experience of the truth of what she radiates. I have listened to two of her audiobooks a dozen times, not because I did not understand them the first time but because of the feeling that I have listening to this profound information, letting it flow into my awareness. I listen, I feel and I smile! —JJ*

PRACTICAL PLAY

There are as many ways to experience the field of the heart as there are infinite potentials and individuals. The following Practical Play can assist you in discovering personal preferences for moving into the state of heart-centered awareness.

I am including a popular quick reference list I provide students around the world. This evolving tool offers several strategies for noticing and experiencing heart-centered awareness. These suggestions may be useful in stimulating your own ability to notice and experience being in the field of the heart on a consistent basis.

There are no limitations when accessing the field of the heart, and similarly, there are no limitations to the infinite methods or strategies for noticing, listening, and speaking from the field of the heart. Being in the field of the heart can be as easy as breathing.

- Breathe in. On your exhale, simply relax your physiology. Drop your shoulders and allow your awareness to relax into the center of your being or your physical body. Perhaps you may notice calmness and stillness or even absence of thought. Breathe. Just breathe.
- Ask an open-ended question, such as, "What would I notice if I were to allow my awareness to move back into the heart-field?" or "Where am I in relation to the field of my heart?" Follow that awareness and connect to it, then invite it into your heart. What do you notice? Anything that occurs is perfect.
- Allow for your awareness to move from all thoughts in your head into the field of the heart. This territory spans anywhere from the throat down to the base of the pelvic floor. Sometimes it can be fun to center awareness behind the belly button, imagining there is a circumference of windows surrounding you. The heart-field gives us 360 degree vision.
- Imagine there is an elevator (what I playfully refer to as an e-love-ator) inside your head. See a

miniature version of yourself stepping into the elevator and allow for the doors to close. Press the "down" button. Follow the elevator with your awareness as it descends out of your head, down through your throat, and even farther down into your chest cavity. Allow for the elevator doors to open, and emerge into the empty space, voluminous with potential. What do you notice?

- Take a moment to feel into someone or something you love. Feel that connection. Notice the feeling and allow for that feeling to move through your entire body. Invite that feeling to center in your body, and then ask it to speak to you. What does it say?

- Recognize that the field of the heart is connected to everything. Notice in your awareness that you are not separate—a separate body or being. You are liquid light. Notice that you feel a sense of fluidity. There is no separation between you and everything else. You are present in the here and now and also present everywhere. Ask your heart what it would tell you if you were to listen to it, now.

- Notice the constant flow of thoughts you may be having without attachment to any of them. The more thoughts we have, the less likely we will be to listen to our hearts. See your thoughts as clouds floating on by. Do not attach to the clouds. Observe the cloud thoughts neutrally with a sense of curiosity and without judgment. Observing thoughts and experiences without judgment keeps us in a state of heart-centered awareness.

- Pay attention to True Authentic Desires (TADs). True Authentic Desires well up from the field of the heart and are cues or placeholders by which our awareness gets our attention. Desires are the language of the heart speaking to us. When we listen, we move into a flow where desires become manifestations and experiences.

- Trust yourself. A way to notice, speak, and listen from the heart is to start trusting yourself. The more you develop a sense of trust in yourself, the more your heart will lead in navigating your consciousness. The more you resonate in trust, the more your mind will follow your heart's intelligence.
- Let go of all sense of not being in your heart. Ask yourself, "If I knew what I might notice were I to listen to my heart, regardless of what anyone else might suggest, what methods of dropping into my heart might I discover?"
- Relax. Let go of asking, "Am I there yet?" Every act of asking the question can take us out of the experience. Relaxing actually gets us in the field of the heart, because when we relax our physiology, we naturally return to coherence and a centering in our being.

Love-Sphere

You may choose to allow your heart-field to surround you as a clear, transparent sphere. I refer to this as a Love-sphere. This Love-sphere is an exterior construct representing heart-centered awareness and the counter-rotating torsion fields that intuit information. It is your own personal reality bubble of love. This Love-sphere can expand or constrict according to your preference. As a clear bubble of unconditional love, the Love-sphere can serve as your atmosphere for being in the heart-field and navigating through the world from a space of completion. This is one of my favorite ways to play with being in the heart and living as my own heartist.

Awareness of being in our hearts leads to a softening of self-consciousness. Our sense of being separate is replaced with the experience of connection to all that we notice and experience. We open to compassion for self and compassion for others. We open to our innate ability to create heart-prints, creating our own unique indelible signature, our own mark in the world.

Welcome to the field of the heart. Welcome home. Do you feel expanded, balanced, centered, peaceful, tearful, joyful? Do you feel calm, excited, connected, whole, limitless, authentic, dissolved, resolved, evolved? Whatever has occurred for you, please trust your own experience. Anything you notice is perfect.

Absence Makes the Heart Responder

Sometimes it is easier to notice being in the field of the heart by virtue of noticing what takes our awareness out of our hearts. In other words, *not* being in our hearts can be easier to notice than being in our hearts.

Often I will notice *not* being in my heart more easily than when I am home in my heart as my natural state. It is akin to being a fish out of water. If we were fish swimming in the ocean, we would not really notice the water. Water would simply be our environment, the way things are. But the moment we are taken out of water and are the proverbial *fish out of water,* we find it is difficult to breathe.

As humans, when we leave our hearts (a sea of love and limitless potential), we may feel stressed, anxious, constricted, fragmented, disconnected, confused, or a variety of seemingly unpleasant notions and emotions. Therein rests our opportunity to take notice and to take refuge by returning awareness to our heart space for sanctity and completion. The moment we notice we have left our hearts, we can invite our awareness home. It only takes a moment to notice we have left our hearts and then to return. Simply notice, and in the noticing, choose to return.

Placeholders for Self-Love

What is a placeholder? In mathematics, a placeholder is a symbol used in a logical or mathematical expression to

represent another term or quantity that is not yet specified but may occupy that place later. So the placeholder is
something used or included temporarily, or a substitute for
something that is not known or must remain generic—it
is that which holds, denotes, or reserves a place for something to come later.[4]

All placeholders represent something "in relation to"
something else, whether we are talking numbers, people,
or patterns in consciousness. Simply stated, a placeholder
is a symbol used in place of an unknown value. In the mathematical equation $1 + x = 3$, x is a placeholder, an unknown
number as part of the equation that sums to the whole.
Placeholders are often used to describe part-to-whole relation-
ships.

Love IS the Whole Equation

I define a placeholder as any pattern of information in our
resonant awareness that reflects back some aspect of self-
love as wholeness and completion not yet recognized.

Placeholders literally and energetically hold places in our
awareness. A placeholder may be anything in our personal
perspective reality or collective consciousness to which we
are relating in our lives. A placeholder may be a thought,
emotion, problem, condition, filter, mask, or habituated
behavior. Limitations as placeholders may resemble problems, conditions, and diseases. A placeholder may also be an
opportunity, possibility, or potentiality not yet expressed.
A placeholder may be a person, archetype, structure, or resonant morphic field. Anything and everything in our lives
can be a placeholder for reflection.

All placeholders to which we are relating may be representations for self-love as reflective awareness or the perceived absence of self-love. As there is no external substitute for the inherent love that we are, all placeholders with
which we resonate may serve as mirrors, shining back to
us an aspect of ourselves we may not yet recognize, accept,

integrate, transcend, or transform as part of our inherent wholeness.

Neutral Value

There is value in defining any pattern with which we are in resonance as a placeholder. Why? When the pattern is observed as a placeholder, there is no charge for or against the pattern. It simply is. As placeholders are anything and everything with which we're in resonance in our experience of reality, this term includes the placeholders we perceive as limitations. Perceived limitations are extensions of limitlessness.

A limitation is a pattern with a perceived fixed boundary. Brackets are placed on limitless consciousness, delineating parameters for the expression of potential. When we're resonating with a limitation, that resonant boundary gives shape and form to what may be experienced, but that limitation is still inherently connected to that which is limitlessness. However, unbounded potential is poured forth into a boundary (field) or container that is shaping it as a limitation.

So when we realize that our limitations aren't really even limitations, that they are also placeholders in our awareness, we have more flexibility to navigate through them. We can choose whether we want to expand the brackets, leverage the brackets, or remove the brackets to embrace more of what is available. As the brackets of limitation are merely an expression of the limitless possibility that always exists alongside other equally weighted potentialities, we are free to choose. We are free to determine what value our placeholders will assume in our lives. We can allow our placeholders (PH) to restore our inner sense of balance (PH balance) regardless of life's unexpected disequilibriums.

An advantage to defining anything that we are in relation to (which is absolutely everything) as a placeholder is that it helps remove the charge by virtue of how we perceive the pattern. By defining a pattern as a placeholder, we engage from a place of grace as neutrality. When we are in relation to a placeholder, rather than a problem, we are no longer polarizing the pattern as something we want to fix or change. When the pattern is a placeholder, neutrality enters the equation.

Neutrality, available through heart-centered awareness, is a continuum where all polarities are extensions of unity. Instead of perceiving from a mental vantage point of wanting to fix something (which polarizes to a state of not fixing), neutrality as unity from the field of the heart brings love to the equation. Love IS, and love has no duality or polarity.

The love that IS from the field of heart creates a vortex attractor for anything that comes in contact with it. Neutrality from the field of the heart allows for alternative options to become available. This is because all is available from the field of the heart. The field of the heart does not take situations apart. The field of the heart sees all in completion. That with which it engages becomes a complementary reflection of its own essence.

This concept of placeholder (PH) was a definite game-changer for me. When I realized that I could shift my awareness around perceived challenges, people, or situations and view them from an expanded perspective as placeholders of my consciousness, I no longer felt like a victim of circumstance. Instead, I could take whatever the scenario was that I was dealing with and, via the power of choice, see it as an opportunity for empowerment and transformation within myself.

This also put an end to looking to blame or change others, or blame myself. I couldn't change people, but I did have the power to change up how I viewed them or showed up, thus giving flexibility for the relationship or situation to become something different. By noticing and unhooking from the charge of whatever the PH brought up for me, I could be more neutral and see the issue from other angles. That shifted up the dynamic, so that I could navigate through the situation in a different, more useful manner than I might have done in the past, based on my habituated behaviors. Over time I have experienced my relationships improving into more harmonious forms of relating and being. Now when a PH appears in my path, even though it triggers me, I can observe it as a reflection that offers an opportunity to show up and choose to do it or view it differently this time around. No guilt, just new possibilities. This way, those patterns that I'm entangled with don't need to keep repeating themselves in the same way. I notice now, when bumps in the road appear, I often perceive them differently, as I am different, and I realize how I can glide over them with increasing ease as another layer for growth, transformation, and evolution transpires.

Recently I experienced a "bump in the road," in the form of a car recklessly flying through an intersection and colliding with my car, just as I was starting to turn. They came speeding out of nowhere, and instead of slowing down to stop for the light, which was about to turn red, they accelerated at the last minute. Fortunately, no one was seriously injured, but much to my dismay, the police officer immediately said I was at fault, as they had the right of way, regardless of anything else. I was stunned and felt I wasn't given a proper chance to tell my side. The cop abruptly disappeared without any follow-up, aggravating me even more. Even though I was willing to accept partial responsibility, I felt that the other party was absolutely also at fault. Even an eyewitness came to my defense, but to no avail. Over the days and weeks that followed, I was still reeling and also wondering what this new placeholder was trying to show me.

What I did notice was just how much this sense of injustice triggered me and the need to speak out and be heard. I even made a trip to the local police department, just to voice my opinion and frustration, all the while dropping into the field of the heart and trying to stay neutral, even though it didn't change anything. I was advised to pay my fine and appear in traffic court pleading not guilty so that I could at least get the points removed from my license. At this point, I am waiting for my date in court, but what I have noticed is that the whole scenario now doesn't carry the same charge for me anymore, and I've let go of attachment to outcome. I've finally been able to realize that in the greater scheme of things, this incident is really just a blip on the radar. Instead, I have chosen to focus my attention on all the positives and interesting alignments that have come along with this experience:

a. While my insurance rates may go up and I've incurred some major expenses, it's really not that big of a deal, as most importantly, no one got hurt!

b. I feel gratitude for the eyewitness, as well as my friend who came to the rescue.

c. Through a situation that involved perfect timing, I was able to avoid having my car totaled and was able to negotiate getting it repaired instead.

d. I now have brand-new headlights, which are significantly brighter, let alone safer than what I had before, especially with it being dark so early in winter.

e. I finally also had some other paintwork taken care of that I had been putting off.

f. I spoke out and stood up for myself regardless of what the final outcome may be.

g. When I picked up my car from the repair shop, the odometer read 111,111. Alignment.

In additional irony, we made a last-minute decision the other night to take my husband's van as we were heading out the door, instead of my newly fixed car, when a large deer ran into the road, hitting us head-on. We walked away without a scratch and with immense gratitude, as it would more than likely have totaled my car. —NG

PRACTICAL PLAY: From Problems to Placeholders

Now that we have mapped the experience of being in the field of the heart, however it may occur, we are going to switch gears and return to our minds . . . if only for a moment.

Grab a pen and paper in case you want to write anything down. Or you can play any way you choose.

Think of something that is currently happening in your life that you consider a problem. When you think about this problem, notice what thoughts, feelings, sensations, or experiences occur for you in relation to this problem.

Notice whether you leave your heart when you consider this problem. If so, notice what this experience feels like for you.

> **For example:** *I am thinking of a problem I am having with a colleague. As I think of this problem, I feel frustrated, angry, disempowered, not seen, not heard, and taken advantage of. My body constricts and my shoulders tense up. I notice that my consciousness has left my heart and is ruminating about this other person who is several miles away.*

Now, as you consider this problem, give the problem a location in your field of awareness.

> **For example:** *When I think of the aforementioned problem, I notice my attention goes about six feet in front of me.* (Wherever you notice the problem, on or off the body, is totally OK. Simply trust where you notice.)

Now what would happen if this problem were no longer a problem but was rather a placeholder in your awareness? Recall that a placeholder is any pattern of information in your personal perspective reality that you are in resonance with to reflect back to you some aspect of self-love or not loving self not yet recognized.

For example: *When I allow the aforementioned problem I am experiencing to become a placeholder in my awareness, it no longer feels so overwhelming. I become curious about this pattern and what this experience is here to reveal to me about myself.*

Now, drop your awareness back into your heart-field, or center in your Love-sphere. Refer to the prior Practical Play if you need assistance.

From the field of the heart, what do you notice now that is different about this placeholder as you relate it from the field of the heart? What new thoughts, sensations, emotions, or perceptions occur for you from this new all-inclusive vantage point? Do you feel more compassion for yourself and for the placeholder? How has your sense of the situation changed?

You may find it helpful to allow for the placeholder to drop into your heart-field too. Now what do you notice? Has the problem as placeholder seemingly dissolved or evolved into something more manageable?

For example:

From the field of the heart, I realize instantly that I am not being kind to myself and respecting my own wants, needs, and desires. I am permitting this colleague to treat me in a belittling manner.

As a placeholder viewed from the field of the heart, this pattern enables me to see that I need to bring self-kindness to the equation. Suddenly I feel compassion for myself and compassion for the other person.

I choose to bring this pattern as placeholder into the field of my heart.

As I allow for this emerging integration, I realize this placeholder offers me an opportunity to be more

loving to myself . . . and then I can respond in a lov-
ing manner about what I am willing or not willing
to show up for in relation to this colleague. I no lon-
ger feel like I need to react defensively. Instead, I feel
centered in my heart and empowered to relate to the
situation in a new, more liberating way.

What do you notice about the chosen placeholder from the field of the heart that is different for you? What thoughts, feelings, sensations, or experiences occur for you now? Do you feel more neutral or indifferent to the placeholder? How does being in the field of the heart provide you with leverage for interacting with the pattern?

If you chose to bring the placeholder into your heart-field, what do you notice now as a result of this integration? What possible options for creating and relating to yourself and the placeholder are now available from the field of the heart? Whatever you experience, trust it. Allow it. Honor it. Congratulations, you have just made a new heart-print.

Nothing Is Normal Too

Sometimes the experience of heart-centered awareness may feel like nothing. Do you perhaps notice nothing when centering in your heart? Noticing nothing or possibly feeling nothing is actually totally normal when connecting with the field of the heart. We are establishing resonant awareness with the implicate part of ourselves that is still potential, not yet expression. So no-thing simply means there is not something, particularly an emotion, thought, or sensation, associated with the heart-field experience. We are, paradoxically, experiencing preexperience.

Allow yourself to notice nothing from the field of the heart. In the nothingness, what wells up from within you? Often what occurs after noticing the nothing-ness and being OK with it is a bubbling up of joy, de-light for the sake of being. This bubbling of joy heralds the recognition of a return to our natural state, for joy is what we are. However, whatever you notice, allow for this to be.

Do not feel compelled to label it or define it. Simply be present to the experience. The more you relax into the practice of heart-centered awareness, the easier it will be to consistently access this state anywhere and anytime.

For me, heart-centered awareness and Joy are what I am and how I choose to live.

This way of being impacts not just me directly but all that I relate to, rippling out to everyone and everything here, there, and everywhere, which in turn ripples back again to me. Understanding some of the physics of the field of the heart, which Melissa so eloquently describes, has helped me understand what it actually means, how it works, and why it is key. Living from the heart doesn't mean I walk around all lovey-dovey all the time and tolerate all circumstances, or that I don't feel "negative" emotions, but it does allow me to approach life from a less judgmental, more compassionate, neutral, and all-encompassing place. I can be OK with who I am, and who others are, imperfections included. It's not something I have to specifically think about "doing" either. It's an innate part of me even when I might not feel like I am there. In any situation, it empowers me knowing that I can tap into the field of infinite possibility and Grace and bring that into the equation.

This is living Joy at the deepest level for me. I can let go of all the arguments, repeating thoughts, uncertainties, fears, and scenarios that go round and round in my head and feel a sense of calm certainty in that still point. I can tap into the ALL thru the field of the heart, where I know that I am always supported by the universe aligned in my best interest. This allows me to "go with the flow" in my life. Even when I feel "stuck" or things aren't going according to "my" plan (or when I can't even figure out a plan!), I know that through the field of the heart, I am access-

ing forces far greater than I am capable of doing with my mind alone. I now notice so many interesting synchronicities that it never ceases to amaze me. I say, "You just can't make this stuff up," because it defies what we've been programmed to believe is possible. As Melissa teaches, I see these signs as cues from the universe that all is in order, even when sometimes it may not look or seem that way. It is often in hindsight that I understand how things have unfolded in their unique perfection. This gives me freedom and less judgment of myself and my current situations. I will often notice how new, interesting opportunities or people will suddenly pop up in my life. And even when things may still appear to be relatively the same on the surface, at the same time, everything can feel completely different! —SN

PRACTICAL PLAY the Joy-Filled Way

Drop down into the field of the heart. Refer to the earlier suggestions for assistance.

As you allow your awareness to center in your heart-field, pay attention to the stillness, the absence of thought and emotion . . . the no-thing-ness. As you observe the no-thing-ness, ask yourself what you might notice if the stillness began to spiral. What direction is this spiral and how do you experience it? Whatever you notice is totally OK.

When this spiraling occurs for me, I notice the experience feels bubbly, tingly, or like a welling up of giddiness. The stillness sometimes spirals into silliness. I feel giddy for no reason whatsoever. I feel joy for no reason whatsoever.

Joy is our natural state, and unlike happiness, Joy is not dependent on external circumstances. We all experience joy differently. To me, joy is connection to our heart-fields, connection to our authenticity as integrity, and connection to something bigger than ourselves, which is still somehow us. It only takes a single reference to catalyze our joy from within. However you experience joy for yourself, trust the experience. Joy is also trust. Trust that the heart of being In-Joy has already been activated. Now the question is, How will you choose to notice Joy as it occurs?

To one who thinks they have never experienced Joy, it is a "that's-very-nice," a distant hankering. That was me, as I embarrassedly confessed to Melissa Joy that I had never experienced this feeling. She lovingly encouraged me to look deep within to access some reference to Joy. It may be an image, a memory, a song, or a long-forgotten feeling. It may even be just the imagination of it. For me, the reference was to a movie I had seen over and over again when I was little and what I imagined the character to be feeling. It was so far removed from my own experience, but it was there. It could be pulled out of the rubble, allowing itself to be examined and then revealed. Shining bright like a diamond. Tangible. Generous. Amplified: the way home to my heart and my connection to eternity. The best gift I could give to myself. Thank you, Melissa, for helping me find it. —PK

5

Heart–Mind Synthesis

There are very few human beings
who receive the truth, complete and
staggering, by instant illumination.
Most of them acquire it fragment by
fragment, on a small scale, by successive
developments, cellularly, like
a laborious mosaic.

—Anais Nin[1]

When I was growing up, there seemed to be two ruling classes in my family: logic and emotions. As my parents had divorced, logic was king in my father's house, and emotions reigned queen in my mother's domain. Like my parents, the two schools of thought/feeling were at great odds with each other. When in my mother's home, it was seemingly expected that I be emotional about everything lest I be perceived as cold and callous. This was in part because my mom was highly emotive and perhaps unknowingly intuitive.

Conversely, my father was a strong advocate of logic. "Stick to the facts" was his mantra. Think before you act. With a PhD in electrical engineering, he approached reality very methodically and with great precision. He used his mind first and foremost.

Emotions and matters of the heart were not his territory, he would profess, and so he used his mind to navigate through his life. My father expected me to do the
same. He reasoned that this approach would always serve
me well. Whenever I was emotional about a situation, he
would encourage me to analyze the problem and use logic
to develop a solution.

I often felt torn between an inclination to trust my feelings as intuitive hunches and the need to use my mind
to gather facts. I thought I had to choose one way or the
other. I can still remember being able to walk into a room
of strangers and instantly have a sense about the people in
the room. However, I soon learned that this type of behavior was not "logical" or appropriate and that, instead, it
was best stick to the facts that people told me.

Moreover, I remember being able to feel what others
around me were feeling without an understanding of my
own heart's empathic/intuitive nature. I assumed their
feelings were my own, often leading to moody and unpredictable behavior. (We will explore the subject of empathy
in the next chapter.)

Over time, I muted my intuition and amplified my logic.
I began to make choices by discounting or disregarding
my intuitive heart-centered nature (and my emotions)
to instead rely more heavily on logic and analytical data.
Logic felt safer.

In hindsight, I recognize I may have experienced the best
of both worlds, as I was able to make a series of distinctions throughout my life between being in the heart and
being in the mind. Little did I realize then, as I know now,
that my environment was a perfect playground for integration. It was not really an *either–or* choice of heart or mind,
emotion or logic. Rather, the choice was "and," to leverage
both heart *and* mind. We can all choose to leverage both
heart and mind.

Heart–mind synthesis is utilizing the gift of the heart's intuition and the gift of the mind's logic together for a powerful synergy that provides for *anything-is-possible* living.

Infinite potential, intuition, and limitless love are all available through the field of the heart, offering access to a plethora of possibilities. More opportunities as options are available. We have more choices. Yet making decisions becomes progressively easier.

Choice with Discernment

Heart–mind synthesis is the integration of heart-centered awareness, coupled with the intellect, providing for choice with discernment. Choice with discernment means making choices aligned with our heart that reflect our personal integrity. We have more options, and we make better decisions.

When making coherent (unified/undivided/whole) choices from the heart that feel right and true for us, we can then make congruent choices that reflect integrity in action. Congruency means that our choices and actions are aligned with our heart-terms.

Minding Matters with Logic

Logic is defined as a tool to develop reasonable conclusions based on a given set of data. Logic is free of emotion and deals very specifically with information in its purest form. Various types of logic can be employed to make sense of the world.[2]

In science, researchers rely on both deductive logic (top down) and inductive logic (bottom up) to prove a hypothesis is true.

Deductive Logic

In deductive logic, if something is true of a class of members in general, it is also true for all members of that class.

> **For example:** *All persons have a brain. Steve is a person. Therefore, Steve has a brain.*

For deductive reasoning to be sound, the hypothesis must be correct. Deductive reasoning is not always true if the premise is false.

It is possible to come to a logical conclusion even if the generalization is not true. If the generalization is wrong, the conclusion may be logical, but it may also be untrue.

> **For example:** *All women are mothers. Susan is a woman. Therefore, Susan is a mother.*

While this is valid logically, it is untrue, because the original statement is false.

Inductive Logic

Inductive logic is considered the opposite of deductive logic. Inductive reasoning makes broad generalizations from specific observations. In this type of reasoning, we may make observations and distinctions or discern a pattern and then make a sweeping conclusion.

Even if all of the premises are true in a statement, inductive reasoning allows for the conclusion to be false.

> **For example:** *Frank is tall. Frank is an artist. Therefore, all artists are tall.*

The conclusion follows logically from the statements but is not true.

In science, there is a constant interplay between inductive logic (based on observations) and deductive logic (based on hypothesis). In everyday life, many of us may employ forms of deductive and inductive logic. However, often we rely on abductive logic to make sense of our world and to make decisions.

Abductive Logic

Abductive logic usually starts with an incomplete set of observations and proceeds to the likeliest possible

Informal logic is the mode used in everyday reasoning and argument analysis. Informal logic consists of two types of reasoning: deductive and inductive.[10]

DEDUCTIVE REASONING

One type of logical reasoning is deductive. **Deductive reasoning** uses information from a large set and applies that information to any member of that set.

For example:
All houses have front doors.
That structure has a front door.
Therefore, that structure must be a house.
Premise may be true. Observation is true.
Conclusion is sound but may be false.

INDUCTIVE REASONING

Another type of logical reasoning is inductive.
Inductive reasoning uses specific data to form a larger, generalized conclusion. It is considered the opposite of deductive reasoning.

For example:
Yesterday, the phone rang while you ate breakfast at 8:00 A.M.
Today, you will eat breakfast at 8:00 A.M.
Therefore, the phone will ring at 8:00 A.M.
Premise is true. Logic is sound. Conclusion is false.

ABDUCTIVE REASONING

Abductive reasoning is a best-educated guess based on partial observation and incomplete information.

For example:
Julie is tired, sad, and lacking motivation.
(observation based on intake form)
People with clinical depression are often tired, sad, and lacking motivation. (partial diagnostic criteria for clinical depression)
Julie has clinical depression. (Maybe or maybe not? Maybe she doesn't enjoy her job, eats potato chips for breakfast, and doesn't exercise?)

conclusion. A best-educated best guess. Still a guess none-theless. Medical doctors often do this in differential diag-nosis. Jurors also rely on this process.[3]

No matter how logical we *think* we are, rarely is our decision-making process based purely in logic. We are not as logical as we think we are when we are making choices. Regardless, when we are employing logic, the process is rarely infallible and may often be based on false premises or incomplete information. Logic only provides us with a close approximation of the truth. Logic is not truth.

Logic is a very useful tool to help make sense of the world around us, but it doesn't necessarily always lead to the truth. Logic helps us to process and organize large amounts of data into meaningful references very quickly. For exam-ple, once we form a reference for a house, with identifying characteristics such as front door, windows, roof, and four free-standing walls, and then label the structure as a house accordingly, each time we subsequently encounter a house, we instantly recognize what we are seeing. House. It would be rather laborious and time consuming if each time we encountered a house, we had to relearn, identify, and label that structure as a house.

Wiggle Room

The brain has a certain amount of wiggle room in that if it encounters a house without a front door (rather, the struc-ture only had a back door), the mind would infer that it is still a house minus one qualifying feature. Or the absence of a front door would not be initially noticed, as the sche-matic reference for a house includes a front door, and so the mind would assume it is there. We fill in the blanks and see the house as a whole.

Consider this meme:

Aoccdrnig to a rscheearch at Cmabrigde Uinervtisy, it deosn't mttaer in waht oredr the ltteers in a wrod are, the olny iprmoetnt tihng is taht the frist and lsat ltteer be at the rghit pclae. The rset can be a toatl mses and you can sitll raed it wouthit a porbelm. Tihs is bcuseae the huamn mnid deos not raed ervey lteter by istlef, but the wrod as a wlohe.

Or rather . . .

> *According to a researcher at Cambridge University, it doesn't matter in what order the letters in a word are, the only important thing is that the first and last letter be at the right place. The rest can be a total mess and you can still read it without a problem. This is because the human mind does not read every letter by itself but the word as a whole.*[5]

What we often consider logic is not really logic at all. Rather it is a schema. Perhaps the presence of schemas may account for how we are able to read scrambled words or words with missing letters?

What Is a Schema?

A schema is a mental concept that informs a person about what to expect from a variety of experiences and situations. Schemas are developed based on information provided by life experiences and are then stored in memory.

A *schema* is a cognitive framework or mental concept that helps us organize and interpret information. Schemas can be very useful because they allow us to rapidly interpret vast amounts of information in our environment. However, these mental frameworks also cause us to exclude pertinent information to focus instead only on things that confirm our preexisting beliefs and ideas.[6]

Our schemas lead to perceptual biases. Perceptual biases limit what we are able to observe and sense as reality. We perceive according to our underlying assumptions. Indeed, our schemas form filters that can influence what we can notice, track, sense, and perceive, often erroneously in the name of logic.

Schematic Filters

Schemas can contribute to stereotypes and deeply ingrained discriminatory processes about ourselves, and others, that we may not even be aware exist in our consciousness. Furthermore, any information that does not fit within the schema or bias is discarded. This is perceptual bias. We see what we expect to see, not what is really there. We see things as we are, not as they really are.

Schemas can make it difficult to retain new information that does not conform to our established ideas about the world. Our perceptual biases as filters limit what we may notice and experience. If our filters are polluted with limiting schemas based on fear and recrimination, then our worlds will reflect fear, self-loathing, and limitation.

So what we often consider logical behavior is actually a series of schemas we may be following. Our so-called logic is an apportioned frame of reference based on perceptual filters that compartmentalize our reality.

Intuition Is Logic for the Heart

The intellectual mind, otherwise known as left-brain logic, is somewhat incapable of creating new data of its own. The left brain is primarily capable of sorting data, primarily from encoded molds of the past. However, the intuitive nature of heart-centered awareness allows for us to create and receive information, not from molded past limitations, but from fresh, infinite potentials that are abundantly available in every moment.

The intuition available through heart-centered awareness provides for moving beyond our filters into effectively holoframing our experiences from a space of completion. Holoframing is seeing from a space of completion. Intuition allows for us to access the whole picture.

Intuition has been scientifically defined as "the process of reaching accurate conclusions based on inadequate information."[7] Simply stated, intuition is the ability to trust our hearts without external evidence.

I define intuition as *knowing without knowing how we know*. Intuition is being fully in receivership of information independent of any reasoning process.

Intuition is often thought to be a function of right-brain awareness. The right brain speaks the same language as the heart. The language of the right brain and the heart is that of gestalts, or patterns. These patterns, noticed, felt, and perceived as intuitive hunches, are often correct determinations not based on logical, linear steps.

Whole-Brain Thinking

Consider that the left brain–right brain dichotomy is more myth than fact. This persistent belief stems from research done by Roger Sperry and Mike Gazzaniga in the 1960s. However, current neuroscientific research reveals that function is not tied to a specific area of the brain or brain hemisphere. Rather, function is a distribution network of cells spanning the brain across lobes and *both* hemispheres. So if you consider yourself more left brained, possibly think again. We may all be whole-brained indeed.[8]

Nobody is really totally in his or her left or right mind, not even when we use traditionally left-brain functions. For example, it has historically been believed that language is predominantly a left-brain function. But new research points us in the right direction. Learning language may be a function of the right brain too.[9]

The dichotomy of left brain (logic) and right brain (intuition) may be a construct or schema that seems true when we follow it. Perhaps a closer approximation to the truth is that the brain has holonomic functions, like the heart. The brain has compensatory mechanisms enabling it to continue functioning normally when certain parts are damaged—the very parts assumed to be responsible for that functioning.[10] Curiously, we may be hard-wired for wholeness.

For many decades, the prevailing view in neuroscience was that all brain neurons are present at birth and the circuitry is established within the first few years of life.

Advances in neurogenesis in the 1990s revealed that the brain has the ability to generate new motor neurons throughout life. The field of neuroplasiticity emerged from neurogenesis when it was discovered that new and existing neurons undergo structural and functional changes in their circuitry in response to the way we mindfully interact with our environment.[11]

Antonio Damasio, professor of neuroscience at the University of Southern California (USC) and director of the USC Brain and Creativity Institute, stated in his book *The Feeling of What Happens* that "the brain possesses several different, emotionally directed, problem-solving mechanisms that evolved from past interactions with ancestral environments." However, he also states that "the way we interact with our current environment continually influences neuronal development."[12]

The way we interact with our environment has an effect on our brain's neurons . . . continually!

Rather than segregating the mind, I prefer to consider the intellectual mind as a whole.

Heart-centered awareness transcends the intellectual mind, which tends to reference information based on constructed memory, to be complete, voluminous with potential.

Prescription for Logic

Don't give in to your fears. If you do you won't be able to talk to your heart.

—Paulo Coelho

Sometimes what we consider logic is really feelings of fear in disguise.

For many years, I loved my career in the pharmaceutical industry. I felt like I was genuinely helping people, was intellectually stimulated by the science, and was challenged by the opportunities to exceed goals and earn promotions. I had autonomy, as I did not work in an office; incredible company benefits; and a hefty salary as well. I traveled around the world to meet prominent physicians and even loved my colleagues like close personal friends.

Then, for many years, I no longer loved my career in the pharmaceutical industry. I learned many things inside the profession that did not feel right to my heart. Initially, I reasoned that I was being unreasonable, being too critical, or not seeing the big picture. But my heart was letting me know something was out of alignment for me. I no longer felt the same joy I had during the first decade of my career.

Logically, I told myself that it is normal not to love my job after working for more than ten years. But I had been promoted several times, changed companies several times, and even changed focus from sales and marketing to research. Still, my waning enthusiasm was of concern. I was starting to feel resentment for all the things I previously appreciated. My heart was trying to tell me it was time to consider making a change.

However, my mind would have nothing to do with that idea. My mind, with all its schemas, cloaked my fear of a new career in various forms of logic. "You have worked so hard to get where you are in your career." "You make great money." " All your friends are in the profession." "What else would you possibly do?" "You are too old to start a new career." "It's not that bad. Get over it and grin and bear it." "Do you know how many people envy pharmaceutical careers?"

My heart said, "Please trust me. If you stay, you will be OK. You will be OK no matter what. If you go, you will create an extraordinary new career based on who you really are. You cannot see it now, but this is so very possible. Anything is possible. Do not fear. You are love and limitless potential."

Nonetheless, logic silenced my heart for a few years. During that time, my body began to get sick, and I again reasoned it was because I was working too hard. Yet, it was really because I was hardening my heart to a truth that was beckoning for my attention. I was no longer congruent with the choices and actions I was taking as a member of the pharmaceutical industry.

For me, it took a double-decker red bus at the World Congress of Neurology in London to propel me on a different path. No kidding; I was hit by a giant bus while crossing the crosswalk outside of the Tower of London. My company had rented out the Tower from Parliament for a conference to present data from our most recent clinical trial. Rather than admit that I really didn't want to be there, I managed to get hit by the bus. My logic was that stubborn.

As a result of my temporary injuries, I had a perfect out from my job.

However, it was not without repercussions. How much easier would it have been to have just trusted my heart? If I had listened to my heart, I could have saved myself a lot of pain and misery. We don't need an excuse to listen to our hearts.

We do not need an excuse to trust our hearts.

After I left the pharmaceutical industry, I made a commitment always to trust my heart first and then leverage logic as a complementary extension of heart-centered awareness. I allowed the heart to lead and the mind to follow. My heart never steered me wrong during my transition to my current career. The heart's intuitive innate intelligence will never steer us wrong.

Although it took me a few years to determine what I really wanted to create career-wise, I was always clear on what to do in the next moment. I felt continually guided by my heart's intuition. I became a sponge, learning everything that made my heart sing. I even remember answering a random ad in a free local paper about a part-time job for a very low hourly rate. Something told me I was supposed to look into the position. I called the number, and the woman who answered said the job was already filled but scheduled me for an interview with the business owner anyway. That interview turned into a three-year business consulting position for a coaching and leadership company with a very healthy salary. The owner called me her angel. I simply trusted my heart, for the heart knows new angles the mind cannot see.

Heart-Flow

Many more serendipitous events have occurred over the years as a result of trusting my heart. Often when we follow our hearts and let our minds follow, we experience synchronicities where things align in a meaningful manner. Heart–mind synthesis fosters flow, and flow is the current of infinite potentials.

Heart–mind synthesis is something we can all access. Sometimes it feels comfortable, and sometimes it feels uncomfortable. The discomfort is often the mind trying to use logic to keep us safe. However, as we will learn in the next chapter, often logic is a cloaking device for fear and other emotions. Being able to leverage choice with discernment through heart–mind synthesis is a very powerful way to feel the fear but not let it stop the true callings of the authentic heart. The heart knows. It always knows. Trust the heart, and allow the mind to follow.

> Heart–mind synthesis positively impacted my relationship with my husband. It is inevitable that couples will argue, and my husband and I have always been ones to analyze why we do what we do, to help keep it from getting out of control and work on improving our relationship and communication. What heart–mind synthesis has added to this is that when things occasionally get heated, we are able to take a step back and drop down into the heart. This gives us each the space to be more neutral, see the bigger picture, and be more open to understanding each other's perspectives when we proceed to have a calmer conversation. We are also more readily able to recognize our own patterns and transform them. Over time, this has resulted in us clearing out different layers of stumbling blocks,

so that we don't have to keep repeating them in the same fashion. Our relationship has become much more fluid and joyful as a result of heart–mind synthesis. —GS

Thought Navigation

Our thoughts are not always logical. Oftentimes we have thoughts that make no sense, and so we try to suppress them or deny them. Any thoughts we try to "drive away" we may steer directly into. Consider it useful to let go of judgments around thoughts, realizing that while we may have thoughts, our thoughts do not necessarily need to have us.

So-called fearful thoughts are just thoughts with labels, judgments that prevent our consciousness as thoughts from becoming anything other than how we have defined the thoughts, and often ourselves. When we are judging our thoughts, we are not loving ourselves.

We are not our thoughts. We are so much more than any thoughts we may be having in any given moment. Ask, "What would it be like if I allowed the thoughts I am having to occur without resistance and without the need to steer them away OR hold on to them? Now what would it be like if I chose a different thought free from judgment and filled with love?"

Heart or Head in Charge

It can be useful to make a distinction for yourself between what it feels like to you when leading with the mind and what it feels like when leading with the heart. Personally, when I lead with my mind, it is most often filled with *shoulda-coulda-wouldas* along with a dollop of fear and dread.

Conversely, when I lead with my heart and allow my mind to follow, my experience is often filled with peace, contentment, centering, possibilities, options and opportunities, love, trust, and excitement.

For example:

FACT: *I have two weeks to finish my book.*

MIND: *I should have started writing sooner, or I would have scheduled more time to write, or I could have called my agent and told her there is no way that I will be done by deadline . . . but now it's too late. I don't have a clue how I will fill all those chapters. I am stressed. Arghhh . . . why is it so noisy here? I am hungry. I am sleepy. I wish everyone would just leave me alone. Why am I even writing another book? No-body wants to read about . . .* and on and on and on the mind will ramble.

Or

FACT: *I have two weeks to finish my book.*

HEART: *Trust. The book is already written. All you need to do is open, allow, receive, and choose the words. Remember, it is already done. Relax.*

MIND'S REPLY: *Sheesh, dear Heart . . . then what is the plan? You are all chill. Give me some ideas, not some esoteric baloney. I have a deadline!*

FACT: *I have two weeks to finish my book.*

HEART–MIND SYNTHESIS: *The book is already writ-ten. All that I want to write will flow masterfully. I am adept at tessaring time so I accomplish more than seems linearly possible. I have written three prior books under the same circumstances. My guid-ance has never let me down. I can tune in to the book download channel and scribe to my heart's content. I have plenty of quiet space and sufficient inter-personal stimulation. All is in balance. Trust. Now choose a plan, as many options are suddenly coming into awareness. What feels in alignment leveraging choice with discernment?* I choose the plan that feels right: write two thousand words a day for the next fourteen days. Go to bed early. Wake up early. Remember to have fun in the process. If it isn't fun, the words won't flow. Now take action, and remember, I am amazing!

You are amazing too, and heart–mind synthesis can bring forth this recognition from within you. Heart–mind synthesis provides us with the ability to override our perceptual filters and the limitations of logic to access the expansive innate intelligence that is a function of the field of the heart. Our hearts can track and follow all waves of possibility, while our minds can implement the congruent choices that support the Integrity Effect.

Emotions as Placeholders

I tether most everything I do to personal integrity. This can be awesome and expansive when I feel great about a situation, or like a personal hell when I don't and feel guilty.

Melissa Joy asserts that we can view everything—an experience, a thought, a way of being or repetitive pattern—as a "placeholder" in consciousness. Kind of like an address we can either visit or drive by—or a house we can either enter from the familiar front door or perhaps the back. If we really want to shift things up, we can crawl in the window or down the chimney! This perspective shift from heavy and weighty thing that needs fixing to "placeholder" has been liberating beyond measure!

These teachings and her mastery of morphing language into tools for playful, fun games gave me a new, expanded way of interacting with life that can adapt situationally and allowed me to view myself in relation to growth opportunities rather than opportunities to condemn, which keeps me in my integrity.

This year, my husband took his own life in a most violent way. I was home at the time and have been left with the aftermath. The mental parade of "what if's" and "could I, should I've known" has been at best suffocating and at worst crushing.

I've got a lengthy twenty-plus-year résumé of alternative healing and conscious thought trainings and yet couldn't break through the mental, circular games and posttraumatic stress disorder from staying with him while his body completed his exit. In one unexpected moment, I experienced the end of my husband's life, the end of our marriage, and the end of life as I'd known it.

My go-tos through this very dark six months have been the teachings Melissa shares.

Sometimes on a moment-to-moment basis, I would remind myself to drop down into the field of my heart and create a heart–mind synthesis. For the initial two weeks or so, that was the best I could do. It was calming and nurturing, and it gave me a sense of control.

Once I got here, then Melissa Joy's perspective of "placeholders" showed up like a beacon of grace. I was able to drop into my heart and view the entire scenario of that day and all associated emotions as placeholders. This perspective gave me the ability to view everything from that day from many different perspectives and without attaching emotion to it. Without this tool, I am certain I would still be locked in the prison of an emotional response rather than the broad perspective of heart-centered, loving grace. Grace for the lens of his perspective, grace that I was able to be with him as he transitioned, the bigger interconnection perspective and the perspective of what can be born from this perceived tragedy. —KM

Seeing Clearly from the Heart

Heart–mind synthesis leads to accurate, intuitive guidance, often referred to as clairvoyance.

Recently I was asked by a new client (a corporate executive) how I am instantly able to see so much about his life and physical body without even knowing him. He was also curious how I was able to influence his state of dis-ease to create well-being (change) from a distance.

I explained to him logically that I simply read the interlocking information codes carried by waveforms in his field (personal perspective reality) and that everyone has the innate ability to read and influence such patterns. We can all be literate in the language of coherence leveraging heart–mind synthesis.

I further provided several different scientific explanations for what he considers clairvoyance, action-at-a-distance, and instantaneous healing. Multiple scientific models support all the aforementioned.

I love the language of science to describe heart–mind synthesis, not to prove that what I do is valid and real but rather as a construct to leverage connection, providing people with congruent maps for understanding unseen terrains.

We can all bridge the local linear effects of everyday life matters with the nonlocal, nonlinear effects of holonomic healing through the prism of science . . . and science makes sense to our inquiring minds. To me, holonomic science severs our sense of disconnection while serving as a scenic route to truth. Truth, like love, is already wholly proven. We can leverage science and logic not to prove that heart–mind synthesis works but to prove that people work as a whole, and heart–mind synthesis supports this resonant recognition.

I love to teach physics to explain transformation. But change isn't rocket science. If we want to experience change, we must make different choices. If we want complete change, we choose from the heart and allow the mind to follow.

Heart–mind synthesis is a tango with the universe, establishing a rhythmic flow with the unified heart of completion and then making deliberate choices that align with new heart-prints.

PRACTICAL PLAY: Heart–Mind Synthesis

Grab a pen and paper if you choose.

Consider a situation, challenge, or opportunity in your life where you currently face uncertainty.

State the Fact of the situation.

> **For example:** *I am considering moving from Denver to New York.*

From the mind's perspective, write down what occurs for you.

> **For example:**
>
> MIND: *I really want to move, but I am worried and fearful. I don't know if I will like it. I would need to find a new place to live, and a new job. I don't know that many people in the new city. It's a hassle to move. I will never be able to pull it off.*

Now, drop into your heart. Refer to chapter 4 Practical Play if you need assistance. From the heart's perspective, write down what occurs for you.

> **For example:**
>
> HEART: *Trust this True Authentic Desire. This move is expansive and fulfilling for you. The new city awaits you. Follow me.*
>
> MIND'S REPLY: *But how?*

Now, utilizing heart–mind synthesis, write down what occurs to you. Remember to drop into your heart first and allow the mind simply to choose from the options the heart will offer.

For example:

HEART—MIND SYNTHESIS: *In my heart, I know without knowing how I know that I am moving to New York. Please show me three specific options for getting there, Option A, B, or C. Out of these possible options I could choose to help me move, which one would lead to the greatest ease, joy, abundance, and peace? What images come to my awareness in relation to this move? Option A presents images of a moving van, friends helping to pack, and a new studio in SoHo.*

Although Option A may not seem like the most logical choice, heart—mind synthesis gives us access to more than logic. We are able to track the whole picture beyond the immediate verifiable evidence. We can then choose to leverage logic to implement the choice that the heart's intuitive intelligence has revealed.

6

TAS, Emotions, and the WE Experience

But feelings can't be ignored, no matter
how unjust or ungrateful they seem.

—Anne Frank, *The Diary of a Young Girll*

Living from the field of the heart gives us direct access to our innate potential and also provides direct access to our emotional intelligence. Heart-centered awareness does not override emotions. Heart-centered awareness includes emotions and enables us to live fully in integrity as our True Authentic Self (TAS).

Integrity

Integrity is authenticity. There is nothing to fear. Integrity is not some external standard that is incessantly beyond reach. Integrity is within us and is not something to earn. Like grace, it is freely available if we choose. Integrity is simply being wholly (who we truly are) without identifying ourselves exclusively through the masks and personas that we may hide behind. Authenticity is not so scary.

Many spend their whole lives running from themselves and hiding inherent greatness behind projections. Waking up to being exactly who we are, with total acceptance, can stop the exhausting marathon of avoidance. In the pause, if only for a moment, there is a meeting of the soul as our unique sole signature begins to express in an entirely new and liberated way. Integrity becomes like breathing. Easy. Integrity, as authenticity, brings forth joy from within. There is nothing to do other than to be. Integrate (into-great), and express from that natural whole state.

Integrity is the state of being undivided within one self—whole. Thus integrity is also integration and synthesis of all the parts of ourselves that we have compartmentalized and segregated, even the parts of our lives that feel fragmented. Living as TAS is a gateway to integrity.

Our True Authentic Self (TAS) does not require the total dismantling of ego and everything that is familiar. TAS enables us to show compassion toward our own vulnerabilities as we choose to show compassion to others. Our TAS embraces love of self in its entirety—perfectly imperfect—even the parts we do not like. As an absolutely unique expression whose core essence never changes, our True Authentic Self is continually transforming, evolving, and letting go of what is no longer useful. Our TAS embraces the moment and says, "Here I am. I am totally present. Right now. I am different than I was a moment ago, and I look forward to who I may be a moment from now too."

Ask yourself now, what would it be like if you could completely love yourself exactly as you are, perfectly imperfect, with all your self-contained perceived limitations? What would you notice, sense, feel, or experience if you embodied your True Authentic Self from the field of the heart?

The principles of M-Joy have given me permission to explore Love for myself, SELF-LOVE. I always assumed I loved myself, but never gave it much thought. Before learning of M-Joy and the Integrity Effect, I mostly just got up every day and went about life. I always felt I had to "grab the bull by the horns" to get things done. Exploring the M-Joy language has softened me and opened my heart in a new, wonderful way. It has taught me to come from my heart space with intention and expansion. Because of this, a magnificent cascade of circumstances has followed. I have learned to embrace me, even with All my messiness, and I now know that it is just fine to be perfectly imperfect! I am gentler with myself, and this allows me to be softer with others. The unnecessary self-doubt chatter has stopped.

These teachings allow me to walk in authentic integrity. THIS gives me FREEDOM to stand in my power, and to expect the same from others. I look at things differently now, always with optimism, and wonder at the possibilities from this awesome space.

I can be in my heart space, choose, shine, laugh, love with boundaries, and truly Know that I am A-OK. —JKI

TAS and Placeholders

The True Authentic Self is our True Self and Authentic Self living cohesively, united as True Authentic Self. Our True Self is our core essence, perfect love, and limitless potential. Our Authentic Self is the part of ourselves that thinks and feels imperfect, flawed and perhaps limited in capability. Our True Self is undifferentiated love as boundless potential, transpersonal in nature, while our Authentic Self is our uniqueness, our individuality. Our True Authentic Self is the synthesis of both, together as one. They are not separate. Thus the limitations (placeholders) of our Authentic Self are extensions of our True Self as limitless potential.

Consider now how you might relate to yourself differently if all your perceived limitations are not really problems to overcome? Rather they are placeholders that are still inherently connected to your innate limitless potential. How might integrating these placeholders with the field of the heart enable you to relate to them differently? What thoughts, feelings, sensations, emotions, or perceptions occur for you now as you connect with True Authentic Self?

TAP Dance

The construct of True Authentic Self cultivates self-love, self-appreciation, and self-accountability, wielding True Authentic Power, all catalysts for the Integrity Effect. True Authentic Power (TAP) is not power over anything or anyone; rather, TAP is an inner stance of grace that recognizes that there is nothing to power over, as all is available. We are complete, commanding choices from the field of our hearts, leveraging heart–mind synthesis. As we reframe limiting placeholders and clear the distorted perceptions altogether, then the joy of being our TAS emerges to express the Integrity Effect.

Thank you. Within the M-Joy teachings, I've become more aware of my inner self, the deep relationship between one's inner world and relating to the world that surrounds me. There is so much power in recognizing that you in relation to yourself ripple out and affect all that surrounds you. It's given me a new way to frame relationships, because I know that there is no change in a situation unless I transform myself first. There's no blame, no shame—just recognizing the value of relating.

A lot of people are recognizing the value of self-love, but no one can teach it. I believe that M-Joy teaches self-love in a way of piecing together what makes you uniquely you. It ties in all of the external situations that have been influencing your life, molding you into the person that you think you are, and then deconstructs them so you can find the pieces that are worth keeping.

Being part of a younger generation, many people my age don't value the meaning of self-care and are looking for external confirmations to fulfill them. I would say that M-Joy has taught me the meaning of valuing myself and how the external influences hold a place, but if I don't re-

late to them from my heart, they don't last. Once I recognized the power of influence, it was easier for me to find out what was true to me and what wasn't. I was able to really find my voice and navigate in the world by my heart, not an external confirmation. —RM

So, what if the thought of being who you really are evokes feelings of fear and/or unpleasant emotions? What if the thought of being authentic feels scary and perhaps even elicits shame, blame, anger, guilt, envy, jealousy, betrayal, resentment, frustration, or manipulation? What if you are afraid to allow yourself to be who you really are because of uncertainty surrounding who that person might be and what might change as a result of living authentically? Maybe you are afraid of being genuinely you because you do not feel worthy of being awesome now? Perhaps you do not believe in who you really are? What if you are afraid to be Love as completion?

> We're taught to be ashamed of confusion, anger, fear and sadness, and to me they're of equal value to happiness, excitement and inspiration.[1]

What if you truly knew that Love is what you are? Love is what we all are. Any thoughts, feelings, or beliefs that say otherwise simply are not true. Rather, these precepts of confusion may be programs we are running, filters based on distorted perceptions, others' projections, and assumed reflections. Love is what we are when we remove the filters that indicate otherwise. Love is what we are even when we feel otherwise. We are not our thoughts. We are not our feelings. We are not our emotions. We are coherent Love.

TAS in Action

For many years I have struggled with being an introvert and needing to be "out there" for sharing my gifts and running my therapy practice. I have always had in the back of my head that if I were more photogenic, or slimmer, or less direct, then it would be easier and things would flow better. I always felt that if people really knew me, they would see my flaws and imperfections and wouldn't trust me. I subconsciously and consciously thought, but tried not to believe, that if people were going to follow me and learn from me, I had to be the perfect model of what I was teaching. Working with the constructs of True Authentic Self and True Authentic Power has provided more freedom in just being me, wrinkles and rolls and imperfections included. I have found people responding and identifying with those imperfections in new ways that allow for deeper connection and more authentic relationships. TAS is changing how I see myself and how others respond to me. Can't wait to see what else changes through this work. —LE

Consider that some of what you may be feeling at times isn't even you but comprises the feelings of other people you know. In addition, some of what you may often feel are the emotional/thought fields of the collective WE. None of these emotions are who we are, or who you are. Rather, these emotions are transient experiences we may be having or that may be having us. Indeed, these emotions can send confusing signals, obscuring us from the truth of our core essence as love, often clouding our perceptions and experiences of self, others, and all that we relate to in our lives.

Living as our True Authentic Self (TAS) in a personal undivided house of consciousness opens us to living cohesively with others in the WE experience. Being able to discern our TAS, our thoughts and feelings from the thoughts and feelings of others, including the collective, is what empowers us to embody the Integrity Effect in the WE experience.

What Is the WE Experience?

I define the WE experience as balanced living with an equal emphasis on service to self and service to others. The WE experience is more than uniting with others in the name of community. The role of the individual in the true WE experience is not diminished for the overall whole. Rather, the role of the whole individual is pivotal and is directly proportional to the role and value of community cohesion. There is an ebb and flow in this symbiotic dynamic; at times the individual is more self-driven than community oriented, and at other times the individual is more service driven and focused on supporting others. Service to self is what enables service to others to sustainably occur. Compassion for self is what allows for true compassion for others. Love for oneself, as an individual, is what allows for love of others to ripple sustainably into community.

The WE experience honors the role of the individual as the catalyst for creative action, imagination, and collective evolution. The "I" matters. Individuals foster Imagination, Ingenuity, Invention, and Infinite potential. While there is no I in WE, there is no true WE without I. Individual I is not separate from WE. Rather, individual I is an extension and expression of WE, and WE is an extension and expression of I. The two are symbiotic and synergistic. Equanimity is a necessary facet of the WE experience and is key to the physics embedded in the Integrity Effect.

Consider that humanity cannot truly thrive together without the unique contributions of the individuals. We must be whole unto ourselves first and foremost and not look to the WE experience for validation or completion. Validation and completion are our individual birthrights. Completion is innate to TAS, and the truly authentic WE experience reflects this inherent truth.

Emotional Intelligence

So how do we recognize our True Authentic Self amid a sea of emotions that are often Wemotions (other people's emotions)? We can leverage heart-centered awareness to attune to emotional intelligence. Emotional intelligence (EQ or EI) is a term created by two researchers—Peter Salavoy and John Mayer—and popularized by Dan Goleman in his 1996 book of the same name. Emotional intelligence is the ability to identify and manage your own emotions and the emotions of others. It is generally said to include three skills:

1. Emotional awareness, including the ability to identify your own emotions and those of others
2. The ability to harness emotions and apply them to tasks like thinking and problem solving
3. The ability to manage emotions, including the ability to regulate your own emotions, and the ability to cheer up or calm down another person[2]

Confusing our own emotions with thought patterns and feelings that may be another person's is very common. The more we embody TAS and the Integrity Effect, the easier it becomes to discern the differences and cultivate our emotional intelligence.

Pay attention to all emotions. Once we learn to pay attention to emotions as signals, we can then develop discernment over the possible origin. We can ask ourselves questions such as, Is this emotion an intuition, or is this a feeling/thought with a charge? Is this feeling mine, or is it coming from someone else?

Emotions Defined

What are emotions? The *Oxford English Dictionary* defines an emotion as "a strong feeling deriving from one's circumstances, mood, or relationships with others: Instinctive or intuitive feeling as distinguished from reasoning or knowledge." So an emotion is defined as a feeling, but what does that really mean?

According to Joseph LeDoux, professor of neuroscience and director of the Emotional Brain Institute and the Nathan Kline Institute for Psychiatric Research at New York University, "it's been said that there are as many theories of emotions as there are emotion theorists."[3]

Evolution of Emotion

Most neuroscientists agree that our feelings began in our reptilian brain, millions of years ago, as part of the fight-or-flight survival system. When in the presence of danger, we would automatically feel fear to signal our attention. Our primal feelings cued us to run or fight as a matter of survival. Feelings were necessary for the survival of the species. Evidence indicates the reptilian emotions preceded the thinking (executive) functions of the brain by millions of years. So first we felt, and then we thought. *Feelings preceded thought.* This notion gives new meaning to the famous French philosopher and mathematician René Descartes's philosophy "I think, therefore I am."[4]

Highly Attuned Sensing System

The center of emotions is controlled by the sensate system of the reptilian brain, which picks up enormous amounts of data, eliciting feeling even before thought. Consider the sense of smell, for example. Smells can evoke emotional responses without thinking. Perhaps you smell cookies in the oven and instantly feel deep love, evoking a memory of your grandma's house when you were young. You recall that your endearing grandma always baked you cookies during visits. The smell of cookies is associated with a loving sensation at grandma's house. The presence of the cookie reference creates the emotion along with the memory. Even sounds, like alarms, create emotional responses before we have time to think why we may feel panic. Some emotions are in response to our thoughts, but not all emotions have origin in thought.

Thought Filters

Thoughts are mental cognitions—ideas, opinions, beliefs about self and the world around us. Thoughts include the perspectives we bring to any situation or experience. Thoughts can act as filters for our point of view and can create emotional responses, particularly when our thoughts are self-recriminatory, repetitive in nature, or challenged by others.

Emotions or Feelings?

So, what is the difference between an emotion and a feeling? While the two terms are often used interchangeably, some scientists propose they are not the same. Antonio R. Damasio, renowned neuroscientist and current director of the USC Brain and Creativity Institute, has spent the past thirty-plus years striving to show that *feelings are what arise as the brain interprets emotions. Emotions* themselves, he posits, are purely physical signals of the body reacting to external stimuli. Damasio states,

> Emotions are more or less the complex reactions the body has to certain stimuli. When we are afraid of something, our hearts begin to race, our mouths become dry, our skin turns pale and our muscles contract. This emotional reaction occurs automatically and unconsciously. Feelings occur *after* we become aware in our brain of such physical changes; only then do we experience the feeling of fear.[5]

So first we emote.
Then we think.
Then we identify, interpret, and label.
Then we feel.
Consider a feeling of "having butterflies in your stomach," the sense of excitement you may feel when you anticipate something great is about to happen. The "excitement" is a description of the emotion flowing through your nervous system, followed by a *thought of "excitement"* that you have labeled as a *feeling* in response to your physiology by virtue of associating that response to an anticipated event.

However, the emotion and the physiology of excitement are virtually identical to the emotion and physiology of nervousness, which, if consistent, can be labeled as anxiety. Our bodies do not know the difference between excitement and nervousness. Rather, it is our mind that interprets the *emotion* through *thought* that is then labeled as a feeling of nervousness/anxiety. Next time you are feeling nervous or anxious, ask yourself if you are really nervous or anxious, or perhaps you are excited about the unknown possibilities that await you beyond the label.

We are wise to flow with our emotions and closely discern our thoughts and assigned feelings. We are wise to limit our labels, for labels limit us. Emotions can serve as powerful placeholders in our awareness. When we identify with the emotions through habitual thought, feeling, and labels, we may miss the opportunity the visiting emotions may be there to present. Our emotions are gifts of awareness that can unwrap our True Authentic Self.

Discerning Emotions

We can leverage heart-centered awareness to determine if an emotion we are feeling is intuition, a feeling based on a prior experience (often a thought with a charge), or someone else's emotions altogether.

In my experience, when I get an intuitive impulse, it will come in with a strong sensation but without a charge. In other words, I don't feel polarized or pulled by the information in a particular direction (toward the impulse or away from the impulse). In that e-motive sensing, there is not a particular thought or feeling (which can be a thought with a charge) associated with the sensation. Rather, the intuition is just information. Pure emotion. Typically I will feel the information in my physical body, as all emotions run through the nervous system. I will then ask from my heart, if I could describe this information, what images, symbols, or streams of thought would come to my awareness?

Conversely, when I am triggered by an event that brings forth a feeling and associated reference, often from a prior experience, I will usually feel a strong charge. I will also often feel the emotion viscerally in my physical body, which has a corresponding label naming the feeling.

More Than a Feeling

According to the late eminent Dr. Candace Pert, molecular biologist responsible for discovering the opiate receptor, and author of the groundbreaking book *Molecules of Emotion,* emotion is *chemistry* that communicates with the entire body. As a pharmacologist, professor at Georgetown University, and researcher at the National Institute of Mental Health, Pert theorized that the mind is not just in the brain—it is also in the body.

The vehicle that the mind and body use to communicate with each other is the chemistry of emotion. The chemicals in question are molecules, short chains of amino acids called peptides and receptors that she believed to be the "biochemical correlate of emotion." The peptides can be found in your brain but also in your stomach, your muscles, your glands, and all your major organs, sending messages back and forth. After decades of research, Pert was finally able to make clear how emotion creates the bridge between mind and body. Candace Pert was convinced these chemicals were the physical manifestation of emotion.

As Pert explained in her book, neuro-transmitters carry emotional messages. "As our feelings change, this mixture of peptides travels throughout your body and your brain. And they're literally changing the chemistry of every cell in your body."[6] Pert's groundbreaking work revealed to the world that as thoughts and feelings change, they literally change up the charge of the molecules in our bodies, affecting the neurochemistry within.

Bruce Lipton, a cellular biologist and author of best seller *The Biology of Belief,* purports that we have significant control over our biology. He claims that with intentions and beliefs, we can "reprogram" our genes and our lives. This challenges the traditional scientific beliefs that genes control life and that illnesses are often caused by genetic dysfunctions. "Cells experience the same life you experience and [cells] can survive outside of your body by living and growing in a tissue culture dish," Lipton adds. "Research reveals that 95% of the time humans use their subconscious mind which is the habit mind programmed from childhood till the age of 6, after which your life is controlled by those habits. While the conscious mind, which we associate with our personal identity, our thinking and reasoning mind, is used only 5% of the time. . . . You can control your genes by influencing your beliefs and personal attitudes. How I see the world and my perception controls not just internal biology and genetic behavior but it controls how I create a world around me, your mind's perception of the world changes the biology and chemistry of your body which changes the cells in your body."[7]

Beliefs and personal attitudes include thoughts. Thoughts are composed of language. Language affects our DNA in more ways than many people realize.

Dr. Peter Gariaev, Russian biophysicist, has proven that DNA functions like language and responds to language. His research has demonstrated that DNA can be programmed like a genetic computer, using language, effectively healing genetic diseases. Gariaev and his team posit that mainstream science misunderstands DNA and is missing key components that could revolutionize healing and longevity. I have personally met with Gariaev in his lab in Moscow, and his work has the potential to positively transform our understanding of DNA, biology, physics, healing, and even environmental factors.

Our emotions, thoughts, beliefs, and even the language we use to talk to ourselves have an influence on our health and well-being. How we feel matters and impacts body matters too, all the way down to our DNA.

Empathy and Highly Sensitive Persons

Empathy is defined as "the ability to understand and share the feelings of another."[8] We are all empathic. Some people are more aware of this aspect of the human experience than others.

Often, when growing up, children feel the emotions of parents and family members without knowing they are not their own. If a parent is often angry, then the child may take on that emotion and assume it is his or her feeling. The child will feel angry without knowing why. If a parent is very fearful, then the child will receive the fear signals and run these emotions through his or her own physiology.

Children are naturally and noticeably empathic, as they have not placed filters on this innate nature. Over time, children may develop strategies to cope with untoward and unidentifiable emotions. They may revert inside themselves, taking on a shy filter or persona, or they may act out the angry or fearful behaviors at unpredictable times. They become victim to their physiology rather than developing a strong sense of their own individuality, with the ability to discern which are their emotions and which are the emotions of others.

For many years, I was unaware of my empathic nature. I did not know where my emotions ended and others' emotions began. This created a lot of confusion for me growing up, as I would often feel moody and required a lot of alone time. My parents thought there was something wrong with me. I actually remember making a choice to hide this empathic part of myself, so that I didn't have to see a doctor. I can only wonder how many children are inappropriately medicated with neuroleptic and mood-stabilizing drugs simply because they do not have a language and structure for understanding their emotions and the emotions of others.

> People are confusing their own empathic response with some overblown idea about group identity. They aren't the same. People are becoming afraid of their own unique and distinct existence.[9]

There is an emerging awareness of a new class of people being labeled/diagnosed with HSP (highly sensitive person). It is estimated that 20 percent of the human population would test positive for what Carl Jung called *innate sensitiveness*. This innate sensitivity has been well researched, and the term *highly sensitive person* was coined in 1996 by Elaine N. Aron, PhD, and explored in her book *The Highly Sensitive Person: How to Thrive When the World Overwhelms You.*

According to Aron and colleagues, as well as other researchers, highly sensitive people process sensory data more deeply due to a "biological" difference in their nervous systems. This is a specific trait that was previously mistaken for innate shyness, inhibition, innate fearfulness, introversion, and so on. The existence of the trait of innate sensitivity was demonstrated using a test that was shown to have both internal and external validity.

Are these people *innately* shy, or is shy a patterned response, a schema to cope with the overwhelming emotional signals affecting the nervous system? Are only some people highly sensitive, or are we all empathic, with differing coping mechanisms for dealing with the bombardment of emotions? While I am very compassionate to the perceived pain and suffering of HSPs, as one myself, I offer the following: empaths are not victims. Empathy is a gift of human connection. We can learn to mind our state. We can learn to distinguish our emotions, thoughts, and feelings from the emotions, thoughts, and feelings of others. Furthermore, we can also function at a very high level, without the need to protect ourselves from life. Minding our state is a facet of living as TAS and is a tremendous benefit of the Integrity Effect.

Empathy/Sympathy Entrainment

When I first started teaching large seminars with several hundred people, I would experience emotional overwhelm. As I was rather adept at "feeling" what other people were feeling, I would track and experience the emotions of the entire group each day and assist people in moving long-standing patterns that were hindering their perceived life experiences. Then, at the end of each day, I would feel pummeled. I wouldn't know if I was depressed, elated, excited, scared, suicidal, or on the brink of stroking out. I had so fully immersed myself empathically in the emotional patterns of group members that I neglected to mind my own state.

For this reason, I developed a very useful distinction between empathy and sympathy. Furthermore, I developed a strategy that enabled me to track other people's emotions without negatively affecting my own inner state.

Many people confuse empathy with sympathy. They are not the same. Thus making a distinction between sympathy and compassionate empathy is relevant and helpful.

As I often share in my teachings, sympathy is entraining in the resonant charge of whatever experience another person may seem to be having or how he or she is behaving. When we are immersed in the experience of what the person seems to be experiencing, there are no other possibility states available. When we are resonating in the person's misery, drama, pain, rigidity—whatever the placeholder is—when we are in the placeholder, that's the only place we can hold. Thus we experience exactly what that person is experiencing too.

Spaceholder for Placeholder

Compassionate empathy is a Spaceholder. In compassionate empathy, we coherently connect to another through the field of the heart. We then align our awareness, noticing whatever it is that someone may be experiencing as a pattern of information as a placeholder in awareness. This placeholder experience exists simultaneously alongside other possibility states.

As a placeholder for another (connection from the heart), we are able to reflect back to the person an expanded awareness that includes the experience he or she is having in the moment. Furthermore, through compassionate empathy, we do not fully immerse ourselves in the person's feeling states. We only sample the patterns of experience.

I have learned that one of the most useful ways to mind my state while still honoring empathy is to run the patterns in front of me rather than through my own nervous system.

How is this accomplished? I create holographic replicas of my self in front of me, where I can sample the emotions of the other persons. In these holograms, I have access to the exact same information in my own nervous system without the challenging impact to my physiology. In any given moment, I am able to calibrate the patterns others may be in resonance with without taking on those patterns as my own. I have shared this strategy with many highly sensitive people, creating new paths for empaths everywhere. If you suffer from the gift of empathy, try this. It can change your life.

Empathy is not a weakness. Empathy is a strength that does not require protection. When we know how to mind our state, leveraging compassionate empathy, we become a vehicle for emotional intelligence and a catalyst for humanity. Heart-centered awareness enables us to access compassionate empathy, while maintaining our center, power, joy, and personal perspective, no matter what emotions surround us.

Where Goes My Ego?

Heart-centered awareness and TAS enable us to create new maps for ourselves (and others), integrating logic, intuition, emotional intelligence, and even ego.

Ego gets a bad rap. Did you know the word *ego* derives from Latin and means "I"? That's what *ego* means. I as in "individual." Sigmund Freud popularized the term *ego* in his infamous psychoanalytic theory:

Freud (1923) saw the psyche structured into three parts, the id, ego and superego, all developing at different stages in our lives. These are systems, not parts of the brain, or in any way physical. According to Freud, the *ego* develops from the *id,* the pleasure seeker which strives for immediate gratification of all desires, wants, and needs. The role of the *ego* is to ensure that the impulses of the id can be expressed in a manner that is acceptable in the real world. *The ego is the necessary component of personality that is responsible for dealing with reality.* The final aspect of personality to develop is the *superego* which provides guidelines for making judgments. According to Freud, the key to a healthy personality is a balance between the id, the ego, and the superego.[10]

Yet, regardless of Freud's emphasis on balance between the three interrelated structures of the personality, the ego has been the target of great ridicule. Many people treat the ego as some cancer in the body that needs to be eliminated or suppressed, as though eradication of the ego would bring forth world peace, let alone inner peace. Over time, the term *ego* has been contorted and distorted to mean selfishness, lack of compassion, narcissism, walking all over others to drive a personal agenda, manipulation, deception, and tyranny. The ego has taken on a persona of its own, like it is some evil character in a horror movie that we have to destroy.

Ego is necessary. Ego is our interface with the rest of the world. We can have an authentic ego that allows for us to confidently put our best self forward. It is our ego that dares us to be seen, to be heard, and to be honored as a unique individual. It is our ego that allows for our imagination to actualize into experience. Ego supports the expression of the individual's own uniqueness. A balanced ego is healthy self-esteem. Our ego can be the face of our inner truth.

Living as TAS in the WE experience entails a healthy dose of self-love and ego/individuality, balanced by equal compassion for others and a commitment to community. Our wants, needs, and desires are every bit as important as the wants, needs, and desires of others.

PRACTICAL PLAY: TAS

Drop down into the field of the heart. Refer to chapter 4 for suggestions. As you move into your heart, allow your awareness to center inside your Love-sphere, the transparent bubble that represents the heart-field. As you center in the Love-sphere, allow for any and all emotions that occur for you to flow though your body. Do not label them.

Now, think or feel into something about yourself that you would like to change or experience differently. It may be a problem or perceived limitation. Whatever occurs for you, trust it.

As you consider this part of yourself that you want to change, what thoughts, feelings, sensations, or experiences occur for you? Write them down if you choose.

How is this problem really a placeholder in your awareness, there to reflect some aspect of self-love (or not loving self) that you have yet to recognize?

Now, as you consider this placeholder from the field of the heart, what would it feel like if you were to integrate this part of yourself with total acceptance, love, and compassion?

How might you relate to this placeholder differently from the field of the heart as your TAS?

For example:

A few weeks ago, I was feeling really "fat." I noted that I would like to lose weight, as I was not happy with my body. As I thought about this problem, I noticed I felt ashamed, embarrassed, and just fat (fat is not a feeling, but that is the word that occurred to me as I felt my emotions). I felt heavy all around. So I wrote this down.

I could have easily substituted "lose weight" for "lose ego," or lose shame, fear, jealousy, etc. . . . (anything we are trying to get rid of, rather than integrate, can weigh us down).

I dropped into the field of my heart. As I considered how this problem was a placeholder in my awareness, I recognized that I had been telling myself that as soon as I lost the weight, I would feel OK. I was playing the weighting/waiting game for myself. Instead of loving myself completely, exactly as I am, perfectly imperfect, I was putting self-love on hold.

So I asked, What would it feel like if I integrated this part of myself and my body with total acceptance, love, and compassion? A big relief. I noted it would be nice to stop beating myself up for a few extra pounds. I am perfectly imperfect, and my weight has no bearing on my self-worth.

Instead of bemoaning what was wrong with my body, I felt inspired to appreciate all the ways my body is really right. Because I chose to feel good about my body, including my so-called imperfections, I was more easily able to listen to what my body needed nutritionally. When I am self-satisfied from a space of appreciation filled with self-love, it is much easier to eat when I am hungry and stop eating when full. My weight is not really a limitation. I realized my weight was an opportunity to embrace self-love in the moment.

I could also see how focusing on my weight and feeling heavy had been a distraction as well as a cue to pay attention. Suddenly I remembered how heavy I always feel right before

I write. I had the same emotional to physical feeling with the last few books I wrote. As soon as I processed the information moving through me and materialized the writing, my body felt normal again. I was weighed down with information and felt "lighter" once I had released it in written form. Sure enough, the perceived extra weight dropped off once I started writing again. At least I didn't have to lose my self in the process.

PRACTICAL PLAY: Not Mine

Discern your emotions from the emotions of people you know or don't know. Drop down into the field of the heart. Refer to chapter 4 for suggestions as needed.

As you move into your heart, allow your awareness to center inside your Love-sphere, the transparent bubble that represents the heart-field and your personal reality bubble. This reality bubble is all you as your TAS.

Now, consider some limiting or distressing emotions/feelings you have been feeling lately. Can you name them? Write them down if you choose. How long have you been feeling this way?

Now ask yourself, Is this emotion my own emotion, or is this emotion someone else's that I am in resonance with? Perhaps it is an emotional field in the collective? Ask yourself now, is this feeling mine, or is this another person's feelings that I am tracking? Notice where your awareness lands as you ask this question.

For example:

I am centered in my Love-sphere, and even though I am in my heart, I am feeling agitated and irritated. I have been feeling this way most of the day. Is this feeling mine or is this someone else's feeling that I am in resonance with? Perhaps it is the collective angst?

When I ask is this feeling mine or is this another person's feelings, I am tracking, and my awareness goes beyond my physical body in front of me but still inside the Love-sphere. This is not my emotion, but this emotion is affecting my state. This is the emotion of someone I know.

If my awareness lands anywhere on my physical body, the emotion is mine.

If my awareness goes behind me, inside my Love-sphere, it is generally a collective pattern. Usually a collective pattern will appear like a net or web coming off of my tailbone or the back of my neck. Once I notice this is not my emotion, I simply need to clear the confusing signals. Saying or thinking "clear-all" from the field of the heart will clear the interference if the resonant emotion is not ours but is inside our Love-sphere.

If the emotion remains following the clearing of the Love-sphere, then the emotion (feeling) is mine, it is my placeholder (and always was to begin with) to explore. Sometimes it will be a combination of me/not me. If any of the emotion remains, I can become curious about this emotion as a placeholder and interact with the placeholder utilizing the prior Practical Play.

For example, when I cleared my Love-sphere, some of the irritation dissipated, but I still felt tense and a little stressed. So I asked, If I knew what this placeholder as resonant emotion is trying to tell me, what occurs for me? The answer I hear is that I think I have a lot on my plate to accomplish in the next month and I am afraid I won't get it all done. I am feeling fear as a placeholder. As I bring this placeholder into the field of my heart, I recognize this is an old feeling, remnants of old maps and programming about not being good enough and feeling incapable of pleasing others. I recognize this feeling comes from earlier imprints when I was trying to please my parents to earn love. From my heart, I listen and hear, "Love is already earned and proven." Instantly, I feel relaxed and a sense of peace. The tension releases from my body, and I sigh. The placeholder no longer holds the same place in my awareness. After clearing the emotions that were not mine, I had the opportunity to integrate the remaining resonant emotion into my heart. All is well.

7

Addictions as Distractions

Whoa, you like to think that you're
immune to the stuff, oh yeah / It's closer
to the truth to say you can't get enough /
You know you're gonna have to face it,
you're addicted to love.

—Robert Palmer

Love. We are all addicted to love indeed. Not just the idea, not just the feeling, but the neurochemistry of love. The experience of love favorably changes our neurophysiology in both mind and body. When we experience love, our body produces its own natural opiates, endorphins, the feel-good neuro-transmitters. Among these chemicals is oxytocin, often called our "love hormone" because of its crucial role in mother–child relationships, social bonding, and intimacy (oxytocin levels soar during sex).

Interestingly, oxytocin has also been shown to mitigate fear. When oxytocin is administered to people with certain anxiety disorders, activity declines in the amygdala—the primary fear center in the brain. As a result, people feel less fearful. Thus exogenous oxytocin, along with other fear-reducing compounds in clinical development, may eventually be used to treat posttraumatic stress disorder (PTSD) and other fear-related conditions.

Addicted to Love

We are hard-wired for love. Our bodies crave love as much as oxygen and water. Many people do not realize that the neurochemistry produced through love is the same neurochemistry produced by the brain while engaging in addictive behaviors. Thus addiction may breed easily in a person starving for love. *Love and addiction have the same initial chemical impact on the body–mind connection.*

According to studies of the brain using functional magnetic resonance imaging (fMRI), the sensation of love is processed in three areas of the brain.

Area 1: Ventral Tegmental Area (Dopamine). The first area is the ventral tegmental area (VTA), a clump of tissue in the brain's lower regions that is the body's central refinery for *dopamine*. Dopamine performs many functions but primarily regulates reward. Winning the lottery can produce a thrilling rush of dopamine. Remarkably, the VTA also becomes active when one feels the rush of cocaine.

Area Two: Nucleus Accumbens (Oxytocin). Thrill signals that start in the lower brain are then processed in the nucleus accumbens via dopamine, serotonin, and oxytocin. New mothers are flooded with oxytocin during labor and nursing, supporting a strong connection to their babies.

According to neuroscientists,

> this association between rewarding experiences and dopamine levels in the nucleus accumbens initially caused many neuroscientists to believe the main role of the nucleus accumbens was in mediating reward. Thus, it is often implicated in addiction and the processes that lead to addiction.
>
> However, since the initial links were made between the nucleus accumbens and reward, it has been discovered that *dopamine levels in the nucleus accumbens rise in response to both rewarding and aversive stimuli* [emphasis added]. This finding led to a re-evaluation of the functions of the nucleus accumbens, and indeed

of the functions of dopamine as a neurotransmitter. The most widely accepted perspective now is that *dopamine levels don't rise only during rewarding experiences but instead rise anytime we experience something that can be deemed either positive or negative.*[1]

Area 3: The Caudate Nuclei (Dopamine). The last major area for love signals in the brain are the caudate nuclei, a pair of structures on either side of the head, each about the size of a shrimp. It's here that patterns and mundane habits, such as knowing how to drive a car or cook spaghetti, are stored.[2]

CAU: Cause to Pause

The caudate nucleus integrates complex emotions and thoughts about love. The caudate nuclei (CAU) are all about making choices, but they are also connected to addictions because of their role in feeling pleasure, relief, and comfort. In many cases, the reason why a person may choose addiction can be buried in the unconscious, but the caudate nuclei of the brain may hold keys to the pattern. Interestingly, studies have shown that people who have damage to the CAU show repetitive and compulsive behavior. They will keep doing a thing over and over again, even though it's unnecessary and doesn't do them any good.[3]

According to neuroscientists,

> the Caudate is also part of the Reward System. It lies in the middle of your head and looks a bit like a medium-sized shrimp—two shrimp, actually, as each hemisphere of the brain has its own Caudate. The caudate and other regions of the striatum have connections to the cerebral cortex, the top, multi-folded layer of the brain with which we do our thinking. It has connections, too, with memory areas and with the ventral-tegmental area VTA. *Indeed, the Caudate integrates*

data from many brain regions. No part of the brain ever works alone, and love is no exception [emphasis added].[4]

Researchers speculate that as all of our thoughts, feelings, and motivations associated with love assemble in the caudate, we experience states of bliss.

We Are All Addicts

To some extent, we are all addicts! We are all addicted to love, and when love is seemingly not available, we will reach for anything as a cheap substitute to produce the feel-good chemistry.

An addiction is something that causes psychological dependence, so it is a mental and cognitive problem in addition to a physical ailment.[5] According to the *Diagnostic and Statistical Manual of Mental Disorders,* an addiction is classified as a dependence. Dependence is "characterized by compulsive, sometimes uncontrollable, behaviors that occur at the expense of other activities and intensify with repeated access."[6]

I define addiction as follows: all addictions are placeholders in awareness that represent an attempt to find True Authentic Self and simultaneously avoid it. The placeholder that the addiction pattern represents serves as a habituated strategy to avoid recognizing self as an infinitely whole, perfect, and limitless being that is having an experience of limitation.

The pattern as placeholder serves as a habituated strategy to look for fulfillment and acceptance of True Authentic Self in something outside of self that is inherently and incessantly empty. In this recognition, there is freedom to recondition awareness and embrace integrity. There is freedom to move from dis-ease to flow in total acceptance—and to choose anew.

Addicts are not the addictions; rather, these people are individuals in resonance with habituated, constricted containers of consciousness that perpetuate a behavioral loop.

Break the connection with the habit, establish resonance with a different, more useful placeholder that is a reflection of love, and the addictive pattern will transform, dissipate, subside, and cease naturally.

The addiction is a bit like looking in the mirror while simultaneously trying to look away. When mired in the addiction, we cannot see ourselves clearly.

To me, addictions are more like a two-way mirror aligned between our TAS and the addictive pattern. A two-way mirror is a mirror that is partially reflective and partially transparent. When one side of the mirror is brightly lit and the other is dark, it allows viewing from the darkened side, but not vice versa.

The addict sees the reflection of self as the mirror image of the addictive behaviors and cannot see anything else. What is reflected is based on the filters of what is being projected—addiction as confusion.

Conversely, the TAS can shine light on the addictive pattern and see clearly through the two-way mirror. TAS can see through the addiction to the truth of the essential self as love.

Love is the only placeholder worth keeping, and self-love is the gateway to freedom from all addictions. Love as the placeholder returns the power of choice and provides liberation from the shackles and confines of addictive patterns that subtract from our well-being.

To engage by compulsion is to cage without compassion. To engage by choice means the experience of the sum total self as a whole being is occurring without the addiction as placeholder. Addiction is not an addition to self. Addiction subtracts us from recognizing our own inherent completion as one love.

According to the preceding definition, we all may be addicted to something. Whether it is drugs, alcohol, food, sex, sugar, shopping, exercise, work, social media, chocolate, drama, or our own story, we are all looking for love, connection, and feelings of completion We are addicted to distractions as placeholders.

Certainly some addictions are more detrimental to our lives than others. Some addictions are even deemed healthy, such as exercise and work. Nonetheless, consider that there is no difference between addictions, as all are attempts to connect to self-love from a space of completion. The consequences and Ricochet Effects may be more pronounced with some addictions than with others, but the core impetus driving the placeholder of addiction is always the same: seeking love.

Sugar High

In many ways, we are conditioned for addictions from a young age.

Perhaps we would receive a Twinkie or Ding-Dong when we finished all our chores? Perhaps when mom was trying to get work done and we were hungry for attention, mom may have innocuously given us a sugar treat to buy herself some much-needed time. This reward system can prime our bodies for addiction as the mind gets double the love pleasure—a treat from mom and a treat for the body. However, treat or trick? Recent research has shown that sugar is eight times more addictive than cocaine.[7]

Both cocaine and sugar elevate dopamine levels in the nucleus accumbens. Prolonged exposure to either causes down-regulation of the dopamine receptors, which means less dopamine becomes available. Over time, more sugar (or drugs) is required to attain normal dopamine levels. This means that, over time, we need processed sugar just to feel normal. We may even be allergic to sugar, which will make us crave it more. We crave what is not good for us too. Recall that dopamine levels in the nucleus accumbens rise in response to both rewarding and *aversive* stimuli.

As we grow older, we may switch our addiction from sugar to drugs and alcohol, which might be more "socially acceptable" under the guise of peer pressure. Or perhaps we may continue to eat sugar and then diet to lose the weight, which could lead those more vulnerable to develop eating disorders. Or maybe carbs are what we crave. Perhaps we give up the sugar but add caffeine, as it helps us study and work. Or maybe we don't think about the soda pop we consume as we spend a few hours playing video games online with friends we have never met.

Social Media Mania

Maybe we think we are clean and free of substance addictions, but we compulsively spend hours a day on Facebook, trolling our newsfeed and other people's sites. We crave the attention we get from our posts and calibrate our self-worth and popularity based on how many likes we receive. Dopamine levels surge every time someone comments on our posts. We may even argue with people who have varying views and find it thrilling when we can get a rise out of a stranger whom we have the power to block.

Perhaps we are plugged in to social media all the time. But not without paying a price. How many real-life friends do we still socialize with in person? Do we substitute real intimacy for the virtual reality of addictive online connections?

A recent University of Copenhagen study suggests excessive use of social media can create feelings of envy. It particularly warns about the negative impact of "lurking" on social media without connecting with anyone. The study of more than one thousand participants says that "regular use of social networking such as Facebook can negatively affect your emotional well-being and satisfaction with life."[8]

Addicted to Drama, Misery, and Negative Attention

Negative attention is still attention, and as we learned earlier, the mind does not distinguish between rewarding stimuli and aversive stimuli before producing endorphins. The dopamine cascade will trigger either way.

Hence many are addicted to patterns that may not initially feel good but persist because of the chemistry that is produced as a result. For some, this can look like ongoing drama, perpetual misery, victimhood, or antagonism. We become addicted to the negative attention that feeds our physiology in the same way a drug rush might occur.

We can often set this up such that other people are the source of our problems. It's their fault we have this drama, disappointment, misery, or discontent. As long as other people remain the perpetual source of our drama, disappointment, discontent, and dissatisfaction with our lives, other people will also remain the source of our peace, joy, happiness, personal power, and fulfillment.

Addiction to drama is false power created as a polarized reaction to feeling powerless. Drama drains our power no matter what role we may be playing back and forth, victim or perpetrator alike. All actors in the drama are directing life force away from the vortex of the heart into the push–pull linear dynamic of surrogate control. Drama is a tug-of-war with self, and that rope will eventually choke any sense of peace, joy, and semblance of unity with all parties involved. Nobody wins the drama game. Let go of the struggle. Choose to let go and play from the unified field of the heart . . . a drama-free zone.

Addiction Affliction

For as long as I can remember, I have had some sort of addiction. My earliest memory is immediately following my parents' separation and eating whatever I could to fill up my sadness. Candy and cookies were a favorite, and often I would sneak them into my room so I could eat them in private. I remember my mom getting upset because when I went to my dad's house, I would have access to lots of junk food in the cabinets. I developed mindless eating based on loneliness, boredom, or just wanting to fill up on something that would help me feel better, loved, complete.

When I became a teenager, I was still eating too much but found solace in alcohol, mind-altering drugs, and even sex to feel better. All were temporary fixes. Then I discovered binge exercising, which was beneficial and deemed acceptable; it built muscles, burned off calories and untoward emotions, and made me look better (so who cares how I felt, right?). Soon my preoccupation with my weight and body image developed into an addiction to starvation. If I was the skinniest one in the room, I felt OK.

Once I got to college, I encountered a smorgasbord of addictive options. Drugs, alcohol, food, parties, boys, studying, sleeping . . . so many choices. It is said that college is the time to try new things, and indeed, I had my fill. But I still felt empty inside.

After college, for two years, I was addicted to work and grad school, with periodic visits from old addictions, augmented by shopping as I reasoned I needed "work clothes" to dress the part. On days when I was feeling down, I would stop at the mall on my way home after work. My finances were a mess because of my marginal propensity to consume. The more I made, the more I spent.

Once I was hired into the pharmaceutical industry, after selling computers for two years, I was focused. This was a serious career. And yet there were many late nights of wining and dining doctors, meetings with colleagues at fancy restaurants, and long banquets to celebrate our company successes. There was a lot of food and drinking and drugs happening on the side. Many of us were taking what we were selling. At one time, I had a warehouse filled with antidepressants and had learned the art of inventory management so that years of samples designated for doctors could find their way into my system undetected. I had my addictions under control.

I was successful at work and soon became addicted to promotions. I was one of the few women promoted to Medical Science Liaison without a PhD. Instead of feeling proud of this accomplishment, I felt shame. It triggered all my feelings of not being worthy. I worked extra hard to hide my sense of not being good enough and consequently ran circles around those with more letters after their names. It was at this time that a moving addiction took front and center. I reasoned that I had to move to advance my career. I would go wherever the promotion took me. But in truth, I was running away from myself, hiding behind a cloak of accomplishments and higher pay grades.

It wasn't until my early thirties, when I met the man I would later marry, that I slowed down and faced myself, and my addictions to everything but self-love. Finally I had somewhere I genuinely wanted to be after work. Finally I had someone who loved me exactly as I was. He didn't care what I did for a living or how much money I made. He just loved me.

When I decided I'd had enough of pushing drugs, he supported my decision to resign. When I didn't know what I wanted to do next, he was encouraging. When I finally figured out what I thought I wanted to do, he loved me enough to let me pursue it, even if it meant changing up our lives together. The whole time I was with this person, I felt like I had a dirty little secret: I didn't love myself. No matter how much he loved me, it still didn't change how I felt about me. And for this reason, it challenged the relationship. I would create problems that didn't exist to try to make him mad at me, to dare him to leave me. Still, he never went anywhere. And neither did the love. Although we eventually separated, in part because I needed to find love within myself, we were able to preserve our mutual love and friendship and only change our circumstances.

Addicted to Company

Many of us are addicted to company. We are not OK being alone. It is important to be comfortable being alone.

I used to not be comfortable being alone and consequently chose compromising company. I would hang with people who were neglectful, selfish, narcissistic, and sometimes abusive rather than face my own fear of being alone. Often, as a means of distracting me from myself, I would choose friends who had various forms of addictions. If only I could help them, then I would somehow be OK, I reasoned. Invariably this codependency resulted in my feeling hurt, betrayed, abandoned, and used.

I learned to stop expecting reciprocal friendship (and love) from people immersed in their addictions. This is akin to expecting the addictions to love us back. Sometimes we need to know when to hold our friends accountable and when to walk away and love them from afar. Love people, not their addictions. Love yourself enough to say No More.

Once I was comfortable with being alone (after uncomfortably trying it), then I was able to connect honestly with myself and find the love that I was seeking, from within. Rather than loneliness, I met my new best friend—me.

We are naturally communal beings. However, to some extent, many have bought in to the WE experience at the expense of the individual I—as you and me completion unto I-self. We have by and large become addicted to company such that even the idea of being alone can put us in a tailspin, in a frenzy, or send us spiraling toward our chosen addictions.

Being alone is not the reason for addiction. Recent research with rats indicates otherwise. Rat Park was a study that demonstrated that rats in isolation were far more likely to become addicts than rats who lived in community. These interesting findings highlight the importance of connection in combating addiction . . . but we are not rats.

We are human beings capable of self-reflection. And we are not at war with addiction. We are at war with our deepest sense of self. It is our sense of self that needs liberating to embrace our own company.

Addiction is not what we are fighting. Rather, we are running from ourselves, often seeking refuge through the eyes of companions or community. It is perhaps only when we can authentically witness our selves, free from judgment and projections, that we find the freedom we are seeking.

Herein rests a key to transcending addictions: being alone and connecting to self. Then we can genuinely connect to others. For me, being alone was Be-in-gal-one. At first I thought *gal* was referring to my gender. But in fact *gal* was in reference to an old French word, *gale,* meaning "merriment." Being alone meant being all one with merriment—Joy—undivided with the essence of ourselves as love in joy.

Traveling Solo

One the greatest ways to move beyond the distractions of our addictions is to take a trip anywhere with yourself. This trip can be a vacation away from your daily responsibilities for a weekend or a week at a time—or it can be for an hour a day. This trip can be lunch or dinner in a restaurant solo or a walk in the woods. Whatever you would normally do with another, just do it with yourself.

At first you may meet resistance, either your own excuses or excuses offered by those around you. As long as you are avoiding yourself through addictions to distractions, there will always be reasons why you can't spend time with yourself. Here is an opportunity to move beyond the placeholder of the excuses into the graceholder of navigating solo.

The first time I traveled by myself, my family and friends were opposed to the idea. They threw out many reasons why they thought I should not go. It would have been easy to acquiesce to their excuses, but the reasons why were all a lie. Traveling with myself was an opportunity to get really clear on who I was, to get comfortable in my own skin and to recognize and appreciate my own company.

If I had known how wonderful solo time (and solo travel) would be in terms of connection to my heart, mind, and body, I would have done it years ago. Alone time is devoid of compromise, comparison, and competition. Completion is easy to recognize when we embrace being alone.

Being alone is hard for many people. Often we will reason this is because of our personality type. We "like" to be around people, as we are extroverts, we reason. Or "being with others is community." Perhaps this is true, and perhaps our personality types and beliefs around community are simply schemas we have developed to justify avoiding being alone.

While connection to others may support freedom from addiction, it is connection to our True Authentic Self that supports the recognition of our inherent completion. Commit to a vacation from company. Travel solo in whatever way you can. It can be a few minutes each day, an hour, or a week. However you travel, know that you have the perfect companion—you. Journey into self-love and take a holiday as a whole day for the joy of being truly you . . . no matter how long that takes.

No Single Moment

If asked when exactly did I know that I finally loved myself and had transcended all addictions for good, I cannot point to an exact moment in linear time. There was no *ah-ha* experience where I saw lightning bolts across the sky and I just knew I deserved to love myself. I think it was a series of distinctions made along the way. Self-loving actions as well as destructive choices combined, which led me to the space of being able to authentically say to myself, "I deserve to love me."

Along the way, a language was formulated to articulate what was in me wanting to come out. It was a matter of dropping filters, and fixed ideas about who I thought I needed to be, so that who I truly was could blossom. It was a willingness to question everything I thought was true. And most importantly, it was a desire and curiosity to be more kind to myself, more kind than the addictions that were draining me rather than fulfilling me. Over time, or as soon as now, the need to hold on to addictive placeholders dissipated until all that remained was myself. Whole. Complete. Free. No shame. No blame. No more excuses. If it could happen for me, I know it can happen for anyone.

Run to Me

Today, running is my meditation, medication, and mediation. For several years daily, I have found solace, soul to sole, in this form of connection to myself, nature, as well as the whole part of me that is bigger than me but is still somehow me in all expressions.

Rain or sun, home or abroad, running is my form of Zensuality, a practical spiritual ritual that enables me not to escape reality but to embrace it. Running is not avoidance. Running (to me) is A Void-dance, a tango with All that Is. There is great Joy in finding stillness within movement and listening to the silence that is voluminous with potential. Running is all that for me, and so much more.

Is running a compulsion or a choice? Running is a choice. I am complete with or without running. This placeholder is a graceholder that adds to the joy of being me. But that joy is present regardless of how many miles I clock, or not.

Addictions create experiences of depletion, not completion. Completion is our birthright, and freedom from addictions is our birthright too. Self-Love is the only placeholder worth being addicted to, and when we have embodied it, we simply don't crave it. It simply is. In this embodiment, we are free to be wholly you and me.

Addictions to Distractions

We are not broken, and neither are our choices. In many instances, we may make choices out of integrity with our inherent wholeness to find a return to wholeness. We may use addictions as distractions. We may choose addictions as a playground for making distinctions, to gain awareness about what we do not want, who we are not, and how we do not really want to behave. We can then leverage the play-ground as a springboard into clarity, to choose a different option, always available through heart–mind synthesis.

> *For me the distraction has become the addiction. When I feel stressed and don't want to do something, like sit down and do the paperwork required to run a business, or record a webinar, or deal with tech issues that appear to be (but are not) over my head, then I used to get up and walk around. I always ended up in the kitchen eating something that I didn't want to and didn't need, but it gave the comfort and distraction from the stress. It became an addiction in many ways. It was my way out of the stress. Using the M-Joy teachings has helped me recognize that pattern. Now I still get up and walk around and sometimes still end up in the kitchen, but I make better choices, like tea or a piece of fruit. Better yet, I don't always end up in the kitchen. I will go tend my plants or just do a few bends and stretches and go back to work and face the stress. Thanks, Melissa, for sharing these teachings in such practical ways. —LE*

Shame Primes Addiction

Regardless of what your fix may be, almost all addictive behaviors carry components of shame. In fact, shame primes addiction.

A key to moving beyond any addictive pattern is to release all shame associated with the pattern. Addiction and shame often accompany each other, and it can be hard to decipher which comes first. We may feel shame and then reach for the addictive placeholder to feel better. Or we may feel ashamed of our addictive placeholder and therefore we reach for the placeholder again to mitigate the shame.

Shame is defined as a feeling of guilt, regret, or sadness that you have because you know you have done something wrong. Unfortunately, shame will trigger all emotions related to lack of self-worth and will leave us feeling not good enough, not worthy, and, most of all, not lovable.

Shame will actually trigger addictive behaviors as a strategy to avoid feeling self-recrimination. In some sense, we may be addicted to shame itself.

Please know there is nothing that anyone can ever do, nothing that you can do, that can stop you from being love. We can't be anything else. Love is what we are. Heart-centered awareness and playing with placeholders can release the shame that binds us. Heart-centered awareness can open us to the self-love that eternally bonds us and offer freedom from addictions.

An important question to ask in relation to any pattern you may be addicted to is, Is this pattern a compulsion, or is this pattern a choice? Is your sense of self and well-being dependent upon this activity, or are you able to maintain a sense of peace with or without engaging in the pattern? Another useful question to ask surrounding addictions is, If this patterned behavior is a compulsion, how can heart-centered awareness, placeholders, and TAS free us from addictions?

PRACTICAL PLAY

Drop into the field of the heart. Refer to chapter 4 Practical Play if you need additional assistance.

While remaining in your heart, consider a pattern or behavior in your life that may qualify as an addiction based on the definition provided herein.

Ask yourself, Is this patterned behavior a compulsion, or is the patterned behavior a choice? Answer honestly from the field of the heart.

In other words, is this behavior something you depend upon for your sense of well-being?

Does the thought of not having access to this placeholder create anxiety, discomfort, agitation, fear, anger, or resentment? Do you feel shame, blame, or secrecy around the placeholder?

If a compulsion, what is the compulsion as placeholder distracting you from recognizing, accepting, or integrating about yourself? Whatever occurs, trust it.

If a compulsion, how can heart-centered awareness and the framework of TAS offer freedom from the addiction? What thoughts, sensations, perceptions, feelings, or experiences occur as this possibility is being considered? Whatever occurs, trust it.

Now consider the placeholder of the addiction from the confines of the mind. Think about this behavior. What thoughts, sensations, feelings, or experiences surface from within the cocoon of the pattern?

Now drop down into the field of the heart. Invite your awareness to release all shame, blame, regret, or resentment that is keeping you shackled to the addiction.

As you relate to the placeholder from the field of the heart, what thoughts, sensations, feelings, emotions, or perceptions occur from this space of loving completion?

What do you notice when whatever you are avoiding through the placeholder of the addiction is allowed to integrate with the heart? If you knew what choice might feel like with respect to this placeholder, what would occur for you?

Ask for Help

Ask for help. Addictions create a sense of isolation and loneliness, which is different than connecting to self when alone as all-one. Seek support from others until you are comfortable solo. Connection with others who are supportive and nonjudgmental is an important component in the movement toward freedom.

The advice provided in this book, and this chapter in particular, can help transform addictive patterns. However, what is being shared also complements specialized formal programs dedicated to addiction recovery. This chapter is not intended to replace professional consultation or treatment, when warranted. You are free to choose and are encouraged to ask for local help to support you in gaining freedom from the shackles of addiction.

8

Integrity, Relating, and the Ricochet Effect

> Real integrity is doing the right thing,
> knowing that nobody's going to know
> whether you did it or not.
>
> —Oprah Winfrey[1]

True Authentic Relating (TAR) is a congruent expression of coherency by our True Authentic Self. True Authentic Relating is integrity in action: clear intent and right relations. TAR is being wholly who we truly are beyond the labels that can define us and confine us.

Integrity in TAR is maintaining an abiding connection to TAS and then relating to others in the same cohesive and connected way. Integrity in the WE experience provides a container for communication and collaboration beyond the masks, roles, and personas we may assume, or be expected to wear, for certain reality structures to function and flow.

True Authentic Relating entails no more compartmentalizing self in relation to others. We are truly the same person, at home, at work, with family or friends, in the community, on vacation, and everywhere. TAR does not segregate our roles, masks, and personas. Rather, all expressions are integrated as one on a daily basis. By being our TAS in all endeavors, we open into TAR and the power of the Integrity Effect.

TAR is a natural outpouring of being in a coherent relationship with True Authentic Self (TAS). When we love, honor, and appreciate True Authentic Self, this creates a congruent alignment with others where we may express that love and honor in all that we relate to . . . as a result, we will attract our tribe; we will attract those who are in alignment with authenticity and living from the heart.

TAR is a reinforcement of self-love, as self IS—as unconditional love experiencing conditions through the created boundaries known as relationship. True Authentic Relating (TAR) is a congruent expression of the True Authentic Self with others and reflects integrity in action.

Off with the Mask

TAR entails discernment relative to masks, roles, and personas as choices, not musts. When we closely identify with masks, roles, and personas, there is often a rigidity of consciousness that accompanies the experience. We may feel bound by that parameter.

When we wear the mask every time we show up in relation to another, we are wearing a projection of who we think we need to be as we relate. As a result, that is all that expresses, and True Authentic Self is cloaked beneath the chosen container.

True Authentic Relating (TAR) is often hindered by the masquerades created for perceived safety. Often we don't know the difference between TAS and our masks. We are not our masks. Masks are choices. Masks are not inherently good or bad. They are constructs of consciousness, schemas that we follow. Indeed, masks can be roles and personas that support us. However, when we think we are the roles or the personas, then we are limited by the confines of the parameters that have been set forth in those roles or personas. As a result, our true identity becomes masked. Thus free authentic expression is often limited through the adorned container.

Heart-centered awareness and True Authentic Relating can support us in moving beyond how we've historically often identified with ourselves: mother, father, lover, wife, husband, sister, daughter, son, executive, housewife, engineer, teacher, victim, healer, and so on.

All these labels are masks, as placeholders, and are not who we truly are. They are roles that we assume and which sometimes consume us.

Many may not know that our roles are placeholders that do not define us or limit us. When we realize our roles are choices, we may choose to experience our roles and personas simply as containers we step into and out of based on the circumstances. They are simply expressions of us, but as expressions, they do not prevent us from engaging in True Authentic Relating as our True Authentic Self. They are shoes we wear, but they are not our soul/sole expression.

The concept of placeholders allowed me to see my dad as a person distinct from me, with his own trajectory and self, and to free myself from feeling trapped by his decisions. For years I believed that I was doomed to repeat his mistakes, and because that was so threatening, I couldn't see the man my dad was—almost up until the time he died. When I became aware that I was using my dad as a placeholder to gain insight into my fears around alcoholism, mediocrity, mortality, addiction, empathy, maleness, family dynamics, etc., I was able to retain my awareness of who I had decided to be in reference to him, and then also get beyond our roles as father and daughter. He is no longer a representation of my fears. He is my dad. I am so grateful that I had the opportunity to see him in a more neutral light while he was still in body, and even more grateful for the strong, clearer connection with him now. A connection that doesn't define who I am or my choices and is based in respect instead of mutual grief. —KS

Family Fair

Perhaps one of the greatest challenges and opportunities for the evolution and expression of our True Authentic Self and True Authentic Relating is with matters of the family. Family affairs are often not fair and equal playing fields for authenticity and the Integrity Effect. It is ironic that the very people whom we are supposed to be the closest to (by virtue of blood) can be the very people we are the most challenged to relate to authentically.

This relative challenge often surfaces as a result of expectations. The expectations of roles to be assumed in family can often consume any opportunity to be wholly who we truly are.

Expectations

Families are breeding grounds for projections and reflections. While there are exceptions, families often come with expectations, roles that can affect how we relate to ourselves and others. It is common for the desires of parents to be projected onto children. Of course Johnny Jr. will grow up to run his father's business. He is a chip off the old family block. Or without question, when little Susan is old enough, she will carry on her mother's tradition of cooking pot roast for the homeless on Valentine's Day.

It is also common for siblings to develop roles of rivalry (or bonding) based on their pecking order in the family. Studies have shown archetypal patterns and behaviors of children depending upon whether they are only children, first born, middle children, or the baby of the family. The birth offer effect is known to affect personality and also career choices.[2] However, even birth order is a role, a placeholder in relation to the rest of the family. Our position in the family constellation does not have to limit how we poise ourselves moving forward.

There is no cookie-cutter approach to True Authentic Relating in family matters. There is no right or wrong way, and how we navigate is deeply personal for every individual. However, choosing to interact from the field of the heart as True Authentic Self can be an empowering way to transcend limitations, expectations, and boundaries that have historically made relating to family a very challenging endeavor.

Get You First

"They just don't get me." This is a common complaint I hear from students and clients around the world as they lament family dynamics. We all have an inherent core desire to be seen exactly as we are, and when family members cannot see us authentically, with total acceptance, the experience may feel painful, like a form of rejection.

However, it is less important for others to see us and accept us as we truly are than it is for we, ourselves, to see ourselves with full acceptance.

Often when it comes to family, which archetypally symbolizes belonging, we will seek acceptance by others at the expense of accepting ourselves. We may hide who we truly are in order to feel comfortable and to conform to family expectations. Or we may rebel against the family expectations to somehow prove we aren't like them. In these ways, we are showing up, following schemas, and defining ourselves by the projections and reflections based on our connection to the family.

Supporting Expectations That Do Not Support Us

I've been aware that I've been running patterns of behavior—habituated responses or creating situations, that could easily define "Groundhog Day" for most of my life. Awareness, however, doesn't always lead to a happy ending or change of said behavior! While attending an M-Joy webinar focused on surrogate power, I had a life-changing, ah-ha moment. I realized that my "Groundhog Day" was simply me operating in the default mode of supporting familial structures and constructs of expectation that supported my family members but did not support me. This occurred as me dummying myself down, agreeing when I really didn't, and being the "fixer" so others would feel good about themselves through the vehicle of my subjugating myself—which I habitually provided, all born of neediness and fear from patterns established in early childhood.

I sat listening and Melissa Joy was employing her unique style of humor, word play, and science combined, which makes any theory accessible. It is her genuine love of people and playful approach to our humanity that allows space for transformative moments to occur!

I had an expanded perspective where I saw I was complicit in creating the "sameness" of all our interactions. I recognized, as unattractive as it was, that I was actually empowered by my false sense of control and self-righteous knowingness of how these family gatherings always unfolded, even though I was left feeling small, not enough and less than. This form of surrogate power, while feeding my "rightness," always left me ashamed later, as it lacks integrity and compassion for self.

In a literal instant, I was able to clearly see several different choices available—all of which would be self-supporting and self-loving. When employed in real time with my family, they didn't go over so well outwardly, but I was left feeling authentically powerful because I stayed in integrity. It's nice to leave the battleground of family without a guilt and shame hangover!

While I continue to act on these powerful realizations, I hold on to a comment—one of many—Melissa Joy made that reminds me to have grace for, and patience with, myself. "Even though you may be done with something, others may still be doing it!" —KO

Being wholly who we truly are without attachment to whether our family "gets us" (or not) opens us to TAR and the possibility family will see us more clearly.

The more clearly and coherently we see ourselves and relate to self, the more this will project and reflect clearly in our interactions with family members. If we are mired in "what do they think of me?" "how do they feel about me?" "why can't they see me?" and are perpetually looking for their acceptance, then there is nobody residing in our own undivided house of self.

Conversely, when we are being wholly who we truly are, and when we are Truly Authentically Relating from a space of completion, without regard for how family members may perceive us or judge us, a space of graceful freedom is created. In our reflection, family members are more likely to see themselves with more clarity and acceptance, and therefore they may see us more clearly too.

Heart-centered awareness and TAR support us in dropping the filters of expectations that we (and our family members) may be looking through. When we let go of expectations, expectations can let go of us.

Reflections of Friends

It is said you can't choose your family but you can choose your friends. Often, through resonance, we will choose friends who mirror back to us a magnificence that we have yet to recognize within ourselves. Friends can also feel like the family we wish we had. Sometimes we will choose friends who will play out unresolved family dynamics and filters. True Authentic Relating fosters friendship of the most authentic nature. In the dynamic of friendship, we have the opportunity to be vulnerable, to find self-acceptance, and to grow our TAS.

Friendship can also spin sideways when emotions such as envy and jealousy are concealed under the mask of friendship. Left unchecked, these emotions can fester and destroy what once was a beautiful opportunity for connection. Pay attention to all confusing emotions that surface in relation to friendship. Allow these placeholders to be explored honestly from the field of the heart. What we may discover will often surprise us. Jealousy and envy are often seeds of unrecognized potential within oneself. Staying in integrity means being honest about how we feel, as confused as it may seem, and allowing those feelings as placeholders to simply be witnessed and honored, so they may potentially transform into the clarity and full expression of self-love.

Frenemies

True Authentic Relating also provides us with the ability to deal with frenemies. A frenemy is a person or group who is friendly toward another because the relationship brings benefits, but harbors feelings of resentment or rivalry.

Frenemies wear many faces, but typical behavior includes not being able to enjoy or support our successes. Frenemies send backhanded compliments, which seem nice on the surface but are laden with insults designed to injure our sense of self. Frenemies also usually talk behind our back in a gossipy manner. While this sounds like high school antics, we can encounter frenemies in our adulthood within our family, among our community, and with colleagues in the workplace.

When encountering this potential pattern, first be honest with yourself: is the frenemy one-sided, or are you also a frenemy to him or her? If so, drop into your heart and ask yourself why you feel you need to behave this way and what gain this placeholder offers you. If it is only one-sided, and the frenemy is truly the sole antagonist, get clear on how you want to handle the relationship. Do you want to confront the frenemy with facts, citing how the behavior is not reflective of a supportive friendship? Do you want to just watch the pattern from the field of the heart and hold space for something to change? Or do you want to move away from any further interactions with this person? Whichever you choose, all are forms of True Authentic Relating, as long as you are being honest with your True Authentic Self.

Frenemies often show up in our lives as an invitation to get really clear on what we are willing or not willing to participate in. Additionally, frenemies can bring forth our conscious and unconscious beliefs about not being worthy or deserving of well-being. Their behavior toward us can allow for deeply embedded beliefs about our lack of worthiness to emerge. These placeholders, when witnessed with compassion, can enable us to transcend the limiting beliefs with a newfound clarity and certainty about the truth of our being. We do not deserve the antagonism, and therefore we will not welcome this form of relating in our house of self. When we hang a no-vacancy sign on our door for frenemies, their hard knocks will soften and they will soon turn away to potentially look within themselves too.

Keeping It Real and Speaking Truth

We all have a natural ability to express the truth of our heart–mind intelligence. We are all capable of and responsible for clearly articulating our thoughts, emotions, and experiences and owning those expressions. Sometimes we don't speak our truth because we're so mired in how another will react to what we say. How another may react is not our responsibility. I am not responsible for how you respond to what I say, and you are not responsible for how I respond to what you say.

We are responsible for our own articulation. We are not responsible for how others perceive our words. Every person's unique perceptual filters will almost always interpret the words differently than intended.

Speaking truth is more for oneself than for anyone else. If we are always concerned about another's reaction to us, then we have left our heart-home, our residence of awareness, to occupy the other person's house of consciousness.

The more we are in full integrity with what we seek to share, the less we may care whether that truth is misconstrued.

As True Authentic Relating (TAR) is not something that requires perfect parameters to occur, TAR can show up in myriad ways. Sometimes TAR may have a delayed sticky reaction where one person speaks from the heart, openly, authentically, and responsibly. The immediate reaction from the "other" might be defensiveness, rejection, or conditioned habit patterns ingrained from the past that appear to be anything other than TAR. Then, a few minutes, weeks, or perhaps months later, there may be a noticeable shift in awareness by the "other," followed by a recognition that it is truly OK to respond differently, authentically, and with total honesty. Remember, honesty and authenticity are for many people a scary place to be. Holding space for safety, which is a function of heart-centered awareness, can be sufficient unto itself for TAR to transpire.

A key facet of TAR is not to be attached to an outcome or how it is supposed to look, feel, or sound. It may feel very uncomfortable in the beginning, simply because it may be unfamiliar. Uncomfortable does not mean it is wrong or not truthful. Uncomfortable may simply mean you and another may be stretching the parameters of communication to encompass your truth as you relate openly in the moment. This stretch may be void of the assumed identities, projections, and personas that may normally adorn you in most interactions.

Keeping it real means keeping it flexible. Do not decide in advance how TAR is supposed to unfold. Allow for your truth to be told. Accept responsibility for your feelings. Remain open to listening to another without judgment. Trust in the process. Notice what is revealed in the communication. Choose to respond in the moment, with a grace and presence of heart that bring love to all encounters.

Choose honesty. Choose True Authentic Relating. Choose love.

Integrity and Speaking Truth

Integrity in relation with others has always been a "no-brainer" for me. You simply show up and keep your word. I'm a trained coach and have coached coaches, and integrity is the gold standard of achievement for living a conscious life. A few years ago, when I recognized I was running the same two patterns of habituated behavior/ response, I recognized it as a personal integrity issue and decided to tackle it head-on. My basic definition of integrity at that time, congruity in thought, speech, and action, lacked boundlessness and fluidity and created the detritus of shame, guilt, and judgment.

Through Melissa's teachings, I've learned that my only lack of integrity is in allowing these judgments of self to define me rather than viewing them as opportunities to play and to show up in full authenticity. By claiming unapologetically my right—my soul purpose—to show up as my truth and then speak and act on it, I AM in integrity even if I make mistakes! So much easier and way more fun, and integrity dictates that as long as my intention is clear and I am expressing authentically, it truly is none of my business how I am received! FREEDOM! —OK

Necessary Roles

True Authentic Relating recognizes that there are certain roles we must play to keep our jobs, run a household, raise children, or travel through an airport. However, no matter what we are doing, we maintain an awareness that the mask or role is not who we are but instead is something we step into to navigate through situations. In the same way, we know when we are driving a car that we are *not* the car; we can recognize our role as a vehicle to support us.

Regardless of our chosen role, we can maintain integrity no matter what comes our way.

The Ricochet Effect

I define the Ricochet Effect as a consequential out-loop of supporting individuals, groups, structures, and circumstances that lack integrity.

The Ricochet Effect occurs as a result of our willingness to show up to help others, and the result brings forth negative circumstances for ourselves. The support ricochets back and hits us in myriad harmful ways.

I have asked what is the deciding factor as to whether giving others a hand up (not a handout) will result in a detrimental impact rippling into our personal perspective reality. In asking this question, an empowering observation has been made, witnessed, and ratified through trial and error in my own life and the lives of students and clients around the world.

Primarily, the difference in whether the Ricochet Effect occurs (or not) is the level of integrity of the person or pattern we are seeking to support. When that person or pattern is in integrity AND genuinely wants to help himself or herself, then the support has a ripple effect that benefits everyone.

Conversely, when out of integrity, when looking to others to do the work, or using the scenario as a form of manipulation to run power, then the circumstances ricochet and reverberate incongruently with a detrimental impact on our own lives and the lives of everyone connected. We become collateral damage.

Collateral Damage

After countless inquiries into Ricochet Effects and surrounding scenarios, this is a very useful distinction that enables anyone to maintain integrity and boundaries without the Ricochet Effects of others' incongruent choices.

This has been a very liberating delineation in awareness. Heart-centered awareness can assist us with being able to discern the difference and supports the ability to choose not to become collateral damage.

Collateral damage is defined as "injury inflicted on something other than an intended target."[3] It has been my experience that when relating to others, if we do not establish boundaries of what we are willing to show up for when others are not in integrity, we experience the Ricochet Effect and become collateral damage.

Ricochet Away

For several years, I was close to someone who was not fully in integrity according to the definition provided herein. This person was very adept at manipulating others and would rarely accept responsibility for the chaos and drama that perpetually occurred in relation to this person's life both personally and professionally.

There was a component of feigned helplessness to the behavior that was a manipulation in disguise, ensuring other people would take care of this person's responsibilities.

Often the chaos and drama would ricochet to those closest to this person, creating untoward circumstances for them. I was one of these people. It didn't matter what day of the week it was, there was always some unexpected mess requiring immediate attention, energy, time, and resources.

The ricochets varied from mild annoyances to full-blown catastrophes, and the consistent variable across all scenarios was the person whom I was perpetually trying to help.

Consistently and wholeheartedly, I showed up for the circumstances, over and over again, reasoning that I could be the one to fix the problems. I was adept at seeing the big picture and also had great attention to detail, so I reasoned I would be the one to correct inequities, sweep things under the rug, and make all the messes go away.

Over time, this pattern of being collateral damage really drained me. I was confused why my life was continually being ricocheted when I myself was coherent and congruent with my choices. I was fully in integrity with being of service and helping out a person seemingly incapable of self-help.

With a little bit of awareness, I had an *ah-ha* moment. As long as I was willing to enable this pattern that lacked integrity, I would continue to experience ricochets and the unintentional consequences, aka collateral damage.

I suppose, in a sense, I was running a form of addiction. I was addicted to being needed, being the one that this person turned to in order to fix what went awry. I thrived on the sense of self-importance that "being indispensable" provided me. As a placeholder, this pattern fed my underlying insecurities about not being good enough, and also a core belief perhaps still lingered from my parents' divorce (if I had been a really good girl, my parents would have stayed together). The corollary in this circumstance was "Maybe if I show up relentlessly, no matter how bad the circumstances, I can fix the problems and prove my worth."

I had temporarily forgotten that love is already wholly proven. I had neglected to recognize that I did not need to don the mask of "fixer" to be of value. My value is inherent. So, too, is yours. Our value as limitless potential is priceless.

With this awareness, I realized I had a choice. I could choose not to change anything and continue to feel used, powerless, and resentfully supportive. Or I could choose to step away altogether. Alternatively, I could choose not to step away but instead to show up differently in relation to this patterned placeholder. I chose to temporarily step away, taking time to get really clear on what I was willing or not willing to show up for, and then stepped back into the relationship with new parameters based on my own heart-terms. Consequently, when I stopped feeding the old pattern, a new pattern emerged that reflected integrity.

Consider that the choices we make matter less than the degree to which we are in integrity with those choices. I was 100 percent aligned with this new configuration, and therefore it worked. Furthermore, others had an opportunity to realign how they were showing up too, including the person who had seemingly instigated the original dynamic.

I Love You AND . . .

Learning to say "I love you and . . . no" is an empowering form of True Authentic Relating. Being able to say to family, friends, colleagues, and even frenemies, "I love you, and if you want to be a part of my life, please stop treating me like a punching bag," "I love you and this is not OK," "I love you and I am not congruent with the choices that you are making," "I love you and yes." If it is not appropriate to show love at work or you do not feel loving, then use the term "I appreciate you AND . . . speaking badly about me at lunch in front of my supervisor is not acceptable behavior."

Many people seem to think unconditional love means sitting back and letting people trample all over us while they meet their agendas. Love does not trample. Love has no agenda. Consider that the notion of unconditional love has been distorted and contorted into people believing that it's OK for people to walk all over one another. All may be love, but not all actions are indeed *loving* actions.

Unconditional love does not mean tolerating intolerable circumstances.

We can be unconditional love while still placing conditions on what we are willing to participate in. Conditions are not placed on the love. Conditions are placed on the circumstances. Love includes the power of choice too.

Heart-centered awareness and living as TAS permit us to stand our ground, commanding love of self while also commanding loving conditions. When we command our conditions from the center of the field of the heart, with integrity as authenticity, our circumstances and conditions will realign to mirror back accordingly.

The M-Joy teaching "I love you and no" has truly changed the way I communicate with my family! The word "and" in that sentence is so important. It has created the space to allow a whole new level of honesty, understanding, and intimacy between me and my husband, my mother, my stepson, and my friends.

In the past, when I haven't agreed with someone I love, I have used the more common phrase "I love you, but no." This has often blown up in my face with the recipient feeling hurt and judged, not loved. It translated more to "Because I don't agree with you or I won't participate in what you want, I don't really love you." This has resulted in both of us not even hearing each other because we become too busy thinking of how best to defend our own opinions, suggestions, or actions in ways that only end up chipping away at trust and intimacy. "But" implies that either my way or yours is right or wrong and the fight begins. Or we are thrown into fear of losing the other person or ourselves and move into damage control by burying ourselves. "And" opens up the possibility that there doesn't have to be a "my way or the highway" impasse. Both ways are simply choices with the charge removed. "I love you AND" is inclusive of your love for each other and for what you each choose rather than exclusive of one or the other. I no longer have to feel compelled to agree to something I feel is wrong for me or make someone I love feel bad if I don't want what they want. I can love them AND say "no, thank you." "I love you AND" has become a gateway to real understanding and the ability to truly hear each other. For me, it has opened a much deeper feeling for those I love, and it has given me the power to speak my truth without fear. —KBS

Sometimes TAR means choosing to step away from situations, circumstances, people, and structures and choosing to love them from afar. We have the power to choose. Love never goes anywhere. Only circumstances change.

When we make a commitment to integrity and to live from the heart, then we may also recognize that not choosing to step away is a choice. Not choosing to step away when a placeholder is abusive or demeaning or nonsupportive is a choice.

While it may feel like a stretch, we can develop Gratitude for Antagonists. The following mantra is something I wrote while still struggling with antagonistic people. I read it every day until I genuinely felt appreciation for the difficult people in my life, including family, colleagues, and frenemies.

Gratitude for Antagonists

I am thankful for various antagonists that have shown up in my life, for they have helped to shape me into an empowered being.

I express gratitude for those who have chastised, criticized, condescended, and ridiculed me. I am appreciative of those who were spiteful, cruel, and vindictive, perhaps to feel better about themselves. I thank them for their manipulation, disdain, anger, jealousy, resentment, and sense of entitlement. For through these experiences, I have learned so much how not to be.

I appreciate being able to see beyond antagonists' misery and confusion to the crystal-clear recognition of truth as love. I am grateful that these experiences did not harden me to myself or to others but rather softened me to an awareness of a potential within us all to transcend the sense of lack and limitation we may perpetuate in relation to . . . everything. I am grateful that I still see that inherent potential for everyone, including antagonists.

I am most appreciative to have learned the power of choice with discernment. True choice. In this recognition, I have learned to say I love you AND no thank you. I love you AND . . . yes. I have learned to choose to recognize joy as an integral part of my being, despite repeated attempts by antagonists to thwart this birthright. Most importantly, I have learned that they cannot truly antagonize me unless I choose to allow it.

I have found clarity amid antagonists' distorted projections—their own limited perceptions. Each time they have cast a blurred lens upon me, I have been invited to see through it, to focus and amplify my own light. Each time the antagonists have been hungry to feed off my life force, I have gained more awareness around my state of being and what True Authentic Power (TAP) really is. I have found grace.

Thank you to antagonists; although you scramble incessantly in not knowing who you truly are, you cannot prevent me from recognizing myself. In the contrast of your confusion, manipulation, and fear, I have found clarity, freedom, and love for my True Authentic Self. Thank you for helping me to see that your antagonism says nothing about me . . . and most everything about you.

If there is any wish I have for antagonists, it is that they begin to see themselves clearly, worthy of creating a different experience, with a willingness to choose otherwise. May they be gifted with clarity, presence, and knowingness of their true essence as love, with peace. I will continue to leave the light on for them as a beacon so they may find their way home. Yet, in my house of consciousness, there is no vacancy for anything other than love.

Heart-centered awareness provides a vehicle for integrity, accountability, and responsibility within family structures, at work, and in relation to community. This follows and expands on the principles of coherency, congruency, and integrity in action, a formula for extraordinary living.

PRACTICAL PLAY

Drop down into the field of your heart. Consider a situation or circumstance in your family or at work where roles are limiting the expression of TAS. Think about the role as a placeholder, and ask yourself what it is there to reveal to you that you have not yet recognized.

What thoughts feelings or experiences occur for you as you relate to this pattern from your heart?

How might you deal with this pattern as a placeholder to enable you to move beyond the limitations of the role to relate from a space of loving self-completion? What actions, ideas, expressions, or conversations might you engage in from your heart?

For example:

My mother has expected that adult children be the ones to initiate contact with parents on holidays if not together in person. As a result, it is always up to me to make the phone call. I never agreed to this schema, nor was it ever discussed. This has been frustrating, because if I didn't call early enough or at a time that was convenient, or if she didn't get the message, I would get ricocheted and she would be upset with me. This would often lead to nasty e-mails, disappointing conversations, and missed opportunities to lovingly connect. I would become collateral damage.

So the last time this happened, I dropped down into the field of my heart and invited myself to see this pattern as a placeholder. As a placeholder, I could see that this pattern was a form of surrogate control—"do it this way because I said so"—and even had a little bit of bullying built in. I could see from my heart that my mom just wanted to talk to me, and by getting hurt if I didn't call on her terms, she had her own ready-made source of feeling empowered as a victim in a distorted way. I could see it wasn't personal, al-

though it felt personal.

   Thus, rather than engage in the old reactive patterns of defensiveness, I chose to tell my mother lovingly from the field of my heart that if she wants to connect with me on a holiday, and I haven't called yet, then please pick up the phone and call me. I would love to hear from her. This was True Authentic Relating, as it enabled me to move beyond the role of obedient child reacting to controlling expectation into a loving space where the pattern could change. The pattern did change.

How might relating from the field of the heart enable you to step into your True Authentic Power, where you can say I love you and NO, or I love you and YES? How can True Authentic Relating assist you with aligning with integrity so that ricochets do not occur? How might you relate to antagonists differently from a space of appreciation, at home, at work, and everywhere you choose?

TAR is a compassionate form of relating that enables us to stay centered in the heart and maintain integrity as TAS, despite antagonistic or bullying attempts to thwart True Authentic Power.

9

Surrogate Power

Supporting Structures That DO (or Do Not) Support Us

> You never change things by fighting the existing reality. To change something, build a new model that makes the existing model obsolete.
>
> —R. Buckminster Fuller

The Integrity Effect opens us to cease supporting structures that do not support us. Heart-centered awareness and commitment to personal integrity enable us to change the patterns within these larger hierarchical models by virtue of how we choose to relate to them. The symmetric physics of equal service to self and equal service to others in realms such as corporations, governments, and all forms of surrogate power structures can close the gaps in these prevailing paradigms.

A movement beyond the gaps through the heart of integrity provides us with empowering tools for relating to and restructuring organizational models at the collective level. Cohesive organizations cannot exist without the integrity of members, including leadership. The ripple effect of integrity within the shared WE experience provides for a new way of relating and creating from unity and limitless potential.

Our sustainable nature can be reflected via group dynamics when integrity is embraced. Integrity, as authenticity, and connection with compassion, offers a hierarchy of collaboration from a space of completion.

All surrogate power structures and paradigms have corresponding morphic field imprints that serve as maps perpetuating the very patterns that may need to evolve. I define a *surrogate power structure* as an organization whose central focus is to create a false sense of dependency for people on the structure for survival. Surrogate power structures typically operate on principles of fear, division, and intimidation.

Morphic Fields

A general understanding of the science of morphic resonance can assist us in understanding how change at the collective level may occur. An understanding of morphic field flow may be applied to evolving new maps at the collective level. Herein rests opportunity to follow the symmetry of love's proportional unity innate to everyone through the field of the heart.

The word *morphic* comes from the Greek *morphe,* meaning "form." The science of morphic resonance can best be understood by studying the pioneering research of biologist Rupert Sheldrake, PhD. Sheldrake has proposed that all of life is dependent on large organizing fields: informational and energetic templates for life, with each species having its own template field. Morphic fields organize the form, structure, and patterned interactions of systems under their influence. Sheldrake theorizes that nothing in the universe is separate, although it may appear separate. That which appears separate and differentiated receives structural and functional marching orders through resonance with morphic fields of information. They are in effect maps or blueprints for life.

According to Sheldrake,

> a **morphic field** is a field within and around a morphic
> unit that organizes its characteristic structure and
> pattern of activity. Morphic fields underlie the form
> and behavior of holons, or morphic units, at all lev-
> els of complexity. *The term morphic field includes mor-*
> *phogenetic, behavioral, social, cultural, and mental fields.*
> Morphic fields are shaped and stabilized by morphic
> resonance from previous similar morphic units, which
> were under the influence of fields of the same kind.
> *They consequently contain a kind of cumulative memory*
> *and tend to become increasingly habitual.*[1]

To me, morphic fields are nonlocal containers of information that organize the experience of reality for all living
organisms. They operate like cloud servers that host data.
When an organism is connected to a particular "cloud" of
information (morphic field), certain experiences are more
likely to occur based on the morphic units (bits of information) contained therein. Morphic fields are like software
programs that provide directions for operating systems at
all levels of life.

Sheldrake continues:

> **Morphic resonance** is the influence of previous
> structures of activity on subsequent similar struc-
> tures of activity organized by morphic fields. Through
> morphic resonance, formative causal influences pass
> through or across both space and time, and these in-
> fluences are assumed not to fall off with distance in
> space or time, but they come only from the past. The
> greater the degree of similarity, the greater the influ-
> ence of morphic resonance. In general, morphic units
> closely resemble themselves in the past and are sub-
> ject to self-resonance from their own past states.[2]

Morphic resonance explains how the presence of the
past affects our future. The memories of prior behavior

and experience (schemas and maps) influence what possibly happens next.

Structured Maps

Morphic fields organize reality. Everything has a morphic field. There are familial morphic fields, social morphic fields, cultural morphic fields, religious morphic fields, political morphic fields, and even economic morphic fields. Paradigms, corporations, and organizations all have their own morphic fields, located within and around the systems they influence. These systems follow the flow of information that is embedded within its corresponding field and contain, in effect, a form of memory of their past. Morphic fields function like outlines guiding the behavior for all organisms and organizations.

Sheldrake contends that because morphic fields are extremely probabilistic in nature, what has happened in the past tends to strongly influence what may happen next.

Sheldrake further explains in *A New Science of Life* that

> whatever the explanation of its origin, once a new morphic field—a new pattern of organization—has come into being, its field becomes stronger through repetition. The same pattern becomes more likely to happen again. The more often patterns are repeated, the more probable they become. The fields contain a kind of cumulative memory and become increasingly habitual. Fields evolve in time and form the basis of habits. From this point of view, nature is essentially habitual. Even the so-called laws of nature may be more like habits.[3]

Change the Current

Morphic field imprints help to explain why paradigm changes may happen so slowly or with great resistance. It is as if there is an invisible hand sketching outlines for what is likely to happen based on what has happened before. However, we can choose to change those lines to be aligned with new heart-prints.

There are two primary ways to change morphic field resonance: either unplug from the field altogether or continue resonating with a field while changing up what we are contributing to it via individual and group heart-centered awareness, thoughts, feelings, and actions. These options are all supported through the Integrity Effect.

Unplugging Altogether

Many people make the assumption that the way to change an existing paradigm is to go up against it, fighting what is wrong to create a right. Wrong and right are a matter of perspective, and morphic fields do not care what we think. However, going up against a morphic field imprint can actually amplify the power of the very field we seek to change. The charge against something serves as polarizing morphic fuel, which further potentiates and amplifies the very information, structure, and behaviors within that field we are seeking to change. Charging against something feeds the isomorphism of that field, creating *more* of the same. Our charge against something creates a current field flow for the very aspect of a pattern or experience we want to change.

It is often more effective to disconnect from a field altogether. Choosing not to resonate with a field is akin to deflating the air in a tire. The shape and form of the tire change and the volume dissipates, while the geometry changes. When we unplug from a field altogether, the shape and form of our experiences change too. Morphic fields are sustained through repetition, functioning like habits. If we stop participating in the habit, our experiential habitat can change.

Contribution to Change

Sometimes it is not practical or realistic to disengage from a morphic field altogether. Perhaps we have a job at a company with which we do not feel totally in alignment. The company culture (also a morphic field) is controlling and very judgmental. Management motivates people using fear, threatening to fire those who don't perform to standards few can achieve. The company does not follow the principles of equal service to self and others. However, it may not be feasible to resign from this position due to fiscal responsibilities at home. Thus we can maintain our job position and simultaneously form a new position in our awareness.

We can change the structure of the morphic field from right where we are through heart–mind synthesis and the principles of the Integrity Effect. A scientist friend of mine once shared with me that he was seeking to change the paradigm of academic science from within. He sensed he had more of a chance to make an impact from *within* the paradigm, and he needed his professorship to pay his bills.

So how do we change a morphic field imprint from within? We practice the very skills we have learned in the prior chapters. We center in our hearts and access neutrality. We see all challenges as opportunities, patterning as placeholders. We curiously explore the placeholders from the field of the heart. We leverage heart–mind synthesis to develop action plans. We pay attention to our emotions and discern what is a thought, feeling, or intuitive hit. And most importantly, we bring our True Authentic Self to work with us, as us, so we can engage in True Authentic Relating. We can choose to resonate in love and to access True Authentic Power and Integrity right where we are right now, and things will change.

Each time an individual changes up his or her thoughts and actions from the field of the heart, there is a morphic unit contribution that is encoded in the fabric of the collective, within a corresponding morphic field. If this thought,

feeling, or emotion is a morphic unit of love and collaboration, with compassion, then morphic fields of love, collaboration, and compassion will become stronger. As they
become stronger, they become increasingly more habitual
and probable and more readily available for others to resonate with them too. In addition, as we consistently resonate in heart-centered fields that follow the principles of
love's symmetry, this changes up the distortions in the
very fields of surrogate power we want to change.

Every individual can change up a morphic field imprint
not by fighting it or trying to change it. Rather, change can
occur by resonating in the heart of integrity and making
congruent choices that reflect proportional unity.

Morphic fields influence our experience of reality more
than we realize. Morphic fields, a natural phenomenon,
also can be deliberately engineered. Consider that many
surrogate power structures utilize the principles of morphic resonance to perpetuate their agendas. For example,
in the pharmaceutical industry, morphic fields are often
deliberately engineered to sell more drugs.

Morphic Field of Depression

When I started marketing antidepressants in the pharmaceutical industry, the average duration of treatment for
depression was approximately six weeks to four months. By
the time I left the profession, the average duration of treatment for depression was more than six months to life. The
average patient now takes antidepressants for 50 percent
longer than he or she did in the 1990s, with some staying
on pills for decades.[4] Depression, as a disease, significantly
increased its longevity through morphic resonance and has
since become a life sentence . . . thanks to the efforts of the
drug companies.

Initially, the treatment of depression was something
that was done exclusively by psychiatrists, who would manage medications, side effects, and the cognitive behavioral

aspects of patients. Licensed psychiatrists were medically trained to diagnose and treat depression.

In 1987, the first SSRI (selective serotonin reuptake inhibitor) came on the market, Prozac by Eli Lilly (my former employer), and changed the way depression was treated. The manufacturer strategically went around psychiatrists and targeted primary care physicians, educating these doctors in how to diagnose and treat depression. Doctors were advised that a chemical imbalance involving serotonin was the cause of depression and that the SSRIs corrected the imbalance. There was no evidence to support this claim, but it was repeated with such frequency that people began to believe it was true. Prozac was a huge success. As additional me-too SSRIs with no greater clinical efficacy soon joined the market (Zoloft and Paxil), multimillion-dollar initiatives were launched by these competing drug companies to grow awareness and increase diagnosis of depression among primary care doctors . . . so more drug prescriptions would be written. Thus the education for treating depression in primary care was driven and performed largely by pharmaceutical companies.

According to the American Psychological Association,

> Prozac opened the floodgates. . . . Since the launch of Prozac, antidepressant use has quadrupled in the United States, and more than one in 10 Americans now takes antidepressants, according to the CDC. Antidepressants are the second most commonly prescribed drug in the United States, just after cholesterol-lowering drugs. Most antidepressants are prescribed by primary-care physicians who may have limited training in treating mental health disorders. In the United States, almost four out of five prescriptions for psychotropic drugs are written by physicians who aren't psychiatrists.
>
> And fewer of their patients receive psychotherapy than in the past. In 1996, one-third of patients tak-

ing antidepressants also received therapy. By 2005, only one-fifth of patients did, according to a study of more than fifty thousand medical surveys that was coauthored by Mark Olfson, MD, professor of clinical psychiatry at Columbia University.[5]

As the number of SSRIs on the market increased, so did the marketing resources of the pharmaceutical industry. Multiple sales forces were deployed to "educate" primary care doctors on diagnosing depression, with as many as three divisions of one company targeting the same doctor at any given time. Direct-to-consumer advertising also targeted unsuspecting consumers, encouraging them (in print ads and television commercials) to ask their doctors about depression and if Prozac, Zoloft, Paxil, and so on, is right for them. The market for depression grew at an astronomical rate.

Were more people being diagnosed with depression because "disease awareness" had improved, or were more people being diagnosed with depression because there were more drugs to sell; because the pharmaceutical industry had carefully crafted strategies and concerted efforts to capture more people in the emerging morphic web of "depression"?

The global depression drug market was valued at $14.51 billion in 2014 and is expected to generate revenue of $16.8 billion by the end of 2020.[6]

Antidepressants are the most prescribed drug for depression. However, very few people realize that the exact mechanism of action of antidepressants is unknown.[7] Furthermore, the underlying etiology of depression is still considered an unknown too.

Did you know there is very little scientific evidence that depression is caused by a deficiency of serotonin in the brain? This was a myth made up by the pharmaceutical industry to sell drugs. Heavy marketing by pharmaceutical companies popularized the faulty chemical imbalance and the SSRI medications used to "restore" it. Over time, this theory gained momentum and almost became accepted fact. Furthermore, the majority of antidepressant studies reveal that SSRIs are no more effective than placebo in the depressed patients.[8]

The morphic field of depression and treatment with SSRIs are now sufficiently established. Treatment of depression with an SSRI has become a matter of habit. It is interesting to ponder the fact that antidepressant use has skyrocketed in recent years, despite a growing consensus that these drugs are dangerous and often ineffective in treating the conditions for which they are prescribed.[9] Researchers have found that commonly prescribed antidepressant drugs, such as Prozac, are actually *addictive* and can wreak havoc with the brain's ability to produce serotonin.

According to *New Scientist,* "after stopping antidepressants, some people get withdrawal symptoms, which can include anxiety, difficulty sleeping, stomach upsets, vivid nightmares, and memory and attention problems. These can last for a few weeks or months."

Antidepressants like Prozac, which are known as selective serotonin reuptake inhibitors, raise levels of a brain-signaling molecule called serotonin, seemingly by blocking a compound that gets rid of serotonin. But after several weeks of taking the medicines, the brain responds by making less serotonin, which may be why when people stop taking them they can get long-term withdrawal symptoms.[10] Doctors sometimes interpret these psychological symptoms of withdrawal as evidence of the return of the original disorder, and so they prescribe *more* drugs to address the problem.

Antidepressants can have their place in treatment of depression, but they are only bandages for the underlying patterns that lead to depression in the first place. And the side effects are not side effects at all. All side effects are still effects of drugs, albeit decidedly inconvenient ones. Freedom from depression is not found in the bondage of antidepressant addiction. Depression is not found in the neuro-transmitters of the brain.

When we close the gap between who we really are and who we think we need to be, how we have been programmed, and how we out-picture those references in our lives, the grooves of depression lift too. When we live aligned with our heart fully with integrity, there is no gap. There is only completion.

Depression is an opportunity to make changes, and sometimes the drugs can help us seize that opportunity to reconfigure our lives. Yet when we do not reflect, introspect, and connect to what our heart and soul are saying, when we instead *only* pop a pill, we are choosing to give our power away.

Depression is a cue that something within a person's life is out of alignment with the truth in his or her heart. In this recognition, depression is a placeholder that warrants our attention. Depression can be a beautiful opportunity for change. Whether we take a prescription or not often matters less than our willingness to show up for ourselves and make some changes.

To unplug from the morphic field of depression, it is quite helpful to disengage from the diagnostic label, as the label establishes morphic resonance with the engineered field of depression. Treat you, not the label of depression that hooks into an engineered morphic field of disease.

Seeding the Market through Morphic Resonance

It is not unusual for pharmaceutical companies to use medical science liaisons to grow a morphic field of disease and influence the prescribing habits of physicians a few years before a drug is approved and available for treatment. When a new neuroleptic treatment (antipsychotic for schizophrenia) was in clinical development, I was hired by a pharmaceutical company long before the drug was approved by the U.S. Food and Drug Administration (FDA).

One hundred twenty-five seasoned experts were recruited from competing drug companies and were deployed as neuroscience disease state specialists across North America to grow the market/morphic field under the guise of "disease awareness."

Our job was to consult with and educate (wine and dine) doctors about the ideal antipsychotic treatment and how to better identify patients suitable for treatment using a typical patient profile. Thus, when the new drug was FDA approved, the medication "conveniently" fit the ideal treatment parameters doctors were primed to accept and adopt into their prescribing habits. Tens of thousands of previously identified patients were converted to the new drug within one hundred days. This drug launch was one of the most successful launches in the history of the pharmaceutical industry, following second only to the launch of Viagra for male impotence.

If you want to witness the making of a morphic field of disease, simply watch what is happening in the realm of obesity. Obesity was recently declared a "disease" in late 2012 by the Centers for Disease Control and Prevention, the timing of which coincided with several new obesity treatments coming onto the market or pending FDA approval. Market value for obesity pharmaceutical treatments is expected to reach a mere $2.5 billion this decade.

Treatment consensus guidelines are being formulated in conferences across medical specialties.[11] These "multistakeholder consensus" conferences are being funded by the very pharmaceutical companies that stand to gain billions from the treatment eligibility criteria. These criteria will determine who will get the drug that many insurance companies will now be forced to fund, lining the pockets of the drug companies.

A new paradigm/morphic field called "Obesity Is a Chronic Disease" is what is being established. Obesity is not a disease by conventional terms. Rather, it is a multifactorial, complex, habituated pattern. Now that the morphic field of obesity as a disease has been instigated by pharmaceutical companies, drugs may be an option, but drugs are not the solution.

Morphic fields, though pervasive, are only probabilistic in nature. This means we still have the power to choose our resonance. We can choose to unplug from a field, or we can choose to contribute new morphic units of heart-centered love to an existing field, thereby changing it from within.

While there may be surrogate power structures that would like to keep us dependent on them for control through the habit of morphic resonance, we have the True Authentic Power to choose. We can relate to all surrogate power structures, whether family, work, or in relation to the larger global community, from the heart, utilizing compassionate empathy and leveraging choice with discernment.

PRACTICAL PLAY: Surrogate Power Structures

Consider an issue or problem you may be experiencing with family, at work, or in relation to the larger global community where controlling parameters are involved.

As you think about this issue, what thoughts, feelings, sensations, or experiences occur for you? Write them down if you choose.

Now, drop your awareness into your heart or center in your Love-sphere, whichever you choose.

From the field of the heart, invite this perceived issue to become a placeholder and give it a location in your Love-sphere if you choose.

If you want to integrate the placeholder into the field of the heart, that is totally fine.

Now, as you relate to the placeholder from the field of the heart, what new insights, thoughts, feelings, or experiences emerge for you? Write them down if you choose.

How is this placeholder as a struggle representing some part of loving yourself (or not loving yourself) that you have

not yet recognized? How might you be more compassionate toward yourself as you relate to this placeholder? How
might compassion toward this placeholder also change the
configuration?

From the field of the heart, leveraging heart–mind synthesis, what options occur for you in terms of navigating
through this opportunity that were not present before this
exercise?

What choices might you make differently, and what
actions might you take with this new awareness?

For example:

*Recently, I was struggling with whether I was going
to continue working with a particular organization.
For a long time, I had not felt fully congruent with
organizational decisions and had reached a point
where I didn't really want to continue the affiliation.
When I thought about this situation, I felt nervous,
afraid, uncertain, and guilty.*

*Then I dropped into my heart and invited this issue
to become a placeholder. As I holo-framed the pattern
from my heart, I could see clearly that the issue as a
placeholder encoded for all the times I stayed too long
in relationships out of a sense of obligation. I could
see how my own pattern of putting my wants, needs,
and desires on hold to meet the desires of others was
playing out with this organization. I could also see
that I perhaps stayed longer than was comfortable
in the hope that someday the organization would see
and appreciate how much I had done for them. I was
looking to them to validate me. Wow. What a big ah-
ha!*

*From the field of the heart, I could see clearly that I
did not need their validation. I was complete whether I stayed or went. My validation is inherent. In an
instant, my placeholder became a graceholder. I was
free. I was free to choose to stay or to go. The decision*

itself mattered less than the consciousness behind it.

I then asked myself, using heart–mind synthesis, "What circumstances and conditions would need to be present in order for me to stay?" I then made a list of heart-terms.

When it was time to address the question of continued affiliation with the organization, I felt clear, strong, and totally OK with whether I chose to stay or to go. I had moved beyond lamenting the past and needing this placeholder to feel complete to an opening where I was complete into myself and I simply knew (without knowing how) that something would be different. Lo and behold, the organization agreed to my heart-terms, and we will continue relating . . . until we don't. Love's freedom flows.

Furthermore, the love and compassion I had shown to myself in relation to the morphic field of this surrogate power structure will change the structure from within. Instead of looking to the structure for love, supporting it more than it supported me, I was able to offer love as completion to the morphic field itself by virtue of first providing self-love from within. This will have a ripple effect that will change the shape of things to come.

PRACTICAL PLAY: Morphic Field

Do you know which morphic fields are playing out in your life that you may wish to disconnect from? Consider a situation or circumstance you would like to change. What thoughts, feelings, sensations, or experiences occur for you as you consider this issue? Write these down if you choose.

Drop down into the field of the heart or center in your Love-sphere. From the heart, ask yourself, if you knew what morphic field you may be in resonance with (either knowingly or unknowingly) in regard to this circumstance, what would occur for you? Often the answer will be multiple morphic fields.

For example, perhaps you never seem to have enough money (a very common plight). You write down: not enough money, stress, worry, anxiety, procrastination, shame, fear.

Consider the origin of this pattern. Maybe you believe you don't deserve to have money? Perhaps your family always struggled financially, and if you are monetarily abundant, it feels like a form of betrayal or abandonment. Maybe you have mixed feelings about money itself, such as "money is evil" or "people who make money are greedy." Is this logical? Is this deductive logic or inductive logic? Where are the holes in this fallacy?

Then drop into your heart or center in your Love-sphere. From the field of the heart, ask yourself what morphic fields you may be resonating with either knowingly or unknowingly. Consider the words you wrote down, as they are cues that function like strings tethering you to a corresponding morphic field. In the case of the money matter, morphic fields of lack, limitation, fear, worry, guilt, and stress are all playing out as limited probability states.

Now, from the field of the heart, how can you change this experience? What morphic fields might be more useful to cultivating more money in your life? Perhaps fields of abundance, joy, action, loyalty (to self), and trust (in self) might support you in a better way. What thoughts, feelings, sensations, or experiences occur for you as you connect to new morphic fields? What choices will you make differently when aligned with abundance now?

How can you notice abundance already playing out in your life? Abundance is about much more than money. Abundance can come in the form of free time, friendship, clean water, great books, and so on. The more ways you notice abundance as it is already occurring, the more abundance will be reflected in your endeavors.

Repeat this exercise as often as needed until you see evidence of new morphic resonance playing out as changes in your life.

10

Fluid Boundaries and Concrescence

Love is the affinity which links and draws
together the elements of the world. . . .
Love, in fact, is the agent of universal
synthesis.

—Pierre Teilhard de Chardin[1]

Concrescence for humanity is possible through the art of letting go. By letting go of preconceived ideas, limiting reality constructs, and rigid notions of reality, we open into the realm of curiosity and creativity where anything can happen. We transform our placeholders to graceholders. By living in our hearts and applying Fluid Boundaries to what appears to be happening, we can move into the gap of the unknown to make new collective heart-prints. There is not just one way to move forward.

Concrescence is defined as "the coalescence or growing together of parts originally separate." The concept of concrescence originated in biology and was later adopted by philosopher Alfred North Whitehead in his book *Process and Reality* as part of a philosophical ontology.

> Every event in Whitehead's ontology is thus a unique combination of *possibility* and *actuality*. The process

of combining the two is imagined by Whitehead to be organic and is consequently called "concrescence." The term concrescence stands for the process that is fundamental for existence. It can be thought of as the growing together of the multiple entities in the world to one single actual entity which then becomes the material for new entities. Because of being organic, a concrescence is different from a mere combination where the whole is the sum of its parts.[2]

According to Whitehead, concrescence can occur through creative synthesis where the act of decision merges the already decided past with the not yet decided future.

Human nature is to look to past experiences to create future expectations. We think things will be a certain way because they were that way before. The presence of the past creates the future. But concrescence integrates past experiences not as predictions of the future but as references only to catalyze new potentials, new probabilities, new creative expressions. Many existing perspectives and models working together will build concrescence.

Consider that concrescence is already occurring in many paradigms when viewed from a heart-centered, vertical perspective. None of the models are absolutely true, but all of the models are relatively true for the scale they are describing.

The scale we use to look at reality matters.

Scale is defined as a range of numbers used as a system to measure or compare things. According to world-renowned Harvard professor of theoretical physics Lisa Randall, "effective theories are keeping track of measurable details without getting caught in unmeasurable components. . . . The speed of light is finite and the universe we know has existed a finite amount of time. This doesn't mean the universe isn't bigger. It is just that we can't make observations beyond that scale."[3]

A Theory of Everything

Wouldn't it be great if we had a theory to explain everything? In physics, string theory is currently under development. This model aims to reconcile quantum mechanics with general relativity and seems to have all the necessary characteristics for becoming a Theory of Everything. It is founded on the principle that matter, energy, and, under certain hypotheses, space and time are manifestations of physical entities below which, according to the number of dimensions they develop in, they are called "strings." For the theory to be valid, physicists propose that there are ten dimensions.[4]

A true Theory of Everything would possibly include all theories, as there is not one ultimate reality. All realities are a matter of scale or, more simply, a matter of perspective. Each model often describes the respective dimension it is observing.

Consider that the evolution of physics and science may simply be an evolution of our perspectives based on scales. Current research builds on and is a logical extension of what is previously known. Current research comes from the past and is based on measurable observations. Aspects of string theory known as super-symmetry and Brane models seem to hold the most promise of being able to build on what is already known and linking to the unknown. However, none of these models can get there alone. They rely on a delicate balance between what has been discovered in the past (predictability) and the unexplained mysteries of the universe (probability).

Predictability

The science of our three-dimensional life is Newtonian physics. Newtonian physics explains how objects obey the laws of gravity. This is the world of physicality and matter. This is a science of *predictability*.

Probabilities

The science of 4-D is a realm of *probabilities.* Traditional models consider 4-D to be space-time, which includes four-dimensional combinations of width, height, depth, and time. Because space consists of three dimensions, and time is assumed to be one-dimensional, space-time must, therefore, be a four-dimensional object. Oxford physicist and mathematician Roger Penrose proposed that space and time themselves are secondary constructs that emerge out of a deeper level of reality. Mathematics professor Andrew Hodges of Oxford University says that "this idea of points of space-time as being primary objects is artificial."[5]

Quantum physics explores an unknown future of probability states. Quantum entanglement experiments reveal that particles can instantaneously communicate over infinite distances. This is a model of a world where everything is connected. At the subatomic level, the reason electrons are able to communicate with each other from thousands of miles away is because they are not separate. Quantum physics challenges our basic ideas about space-time. Relativity from a quantum physics perspective reveals a realm of *possibilities.* This is also a realm of the mind where probabilities can be explored before they fully actualize as experience. We can traverse the past via memories and explore the future through imagination.

However, moving beyond 4-D is problematic for science due to the measurement problem. But nonetheless, there is compelling evidence that there is more than meets the eye, and portals into infinite dimensions may soon be discovered.

Harvard cosmologist and theoretical physicist Lisa Randall posits that there is a hidden fifth dimension that we can't see. According to her widely recognized model, which dovetails with string theory, "the fifth dimension could be so warped that the number of dimensions you see would depend on where you were. . . . The fifth dimension could actually be infinite and we would not have noticed it."[6]

Infinite extra dimensions, depending on our perspective.

Randall has made some astounding discoveries in theoretical physics linking tiny quantum particles to a model of the cosmos. While she utilizes a very pragmatic approach, starting from what science *already has proven,* her colleagues cite her "amazing nose" in terms of knowing where to look for hidden variables. She has a knowing without knowing how she knows, and her intuitive hunches consistently enable her to follow her nose (knows).

Consider that dimensions are simply the different facets of what we perceive to be reality. We are aware of the three dimensions that surround us—length, width, and depth—because we can see them in everyday life. String theory proposes that beyond these three dimensions are additional dimensions that are not immediately apparent to us but that can be still be perceived as having a direct effect on the universe and reality as we know it.

Heart of Hidden Dimensions

Consider that that hidden fifth dimension, too small to measure and too vast to quantify, can possibly be found without measuring devices and mathematical computations. This hidden dimension is found in the field of the heart.

The field of the heart is the gateway to infinite potential and infinite expression, as well as infinite dimensions,[7] beyond the realities we can see and measure into the realm of the unknown. The heart-field is where predictability meets boundless possibility.

The heart-field is the timeless transformative treasure that moves us beyond past experiential patterns of linear time into the holofractal realm of new patterned potentials; we are able to move up, down, right, and left, any which way in all dimensions, esoterically and practically, for they are one and the same from the field of the heart. Vertical and horizontal awareness meets perpendicular planes of possibilities simultaneously.

As we learned in chapter 4, the field of the heart is a counterrotating torsion field or tube torus. Torsion fields are instantaneous signal transmitters and receivers linking local linear effects with nonlocal, nonlinear reality. Our heart-field enables us to traverse all axes of reality from zero-point to all points of perspectives inclusively.

The heart-field is where infinite potentials meet infinite expressions. Infinite perspectives. Infinite choices. Infinite dimensions.

Curiously enough, the physics of heart-centered awareness, a physics of torsion fields, would conceivably enable scientists to reconcile electromagnetism and gravity and would enable mainstream science to prove the existence of unknown dimensions. More than 4,000 papers have been published by more than 150 teams of scientists in the past 120 years describing what a torsion field is, what function it performs, how it works, and where it may be located. Despite this fact, widespread scientific knowledge of this critical, fundamental aspect of physics and biology has been almost *completely excluded* from the world of academic scientists and mainstream research institutions.[8]

Torsion fields or scalar waves are still considered "fringe science." Part of the reason for this is that torsion fields are characteristically supraluminal; they travel faster than the speed of light. Because our measuring devices are based on the electromagnetic spectrum and these tools (based on light) cannot go faster than the speed of light itself, we can't measure torsion fields. However, we can measure the effects of torsion fields.[9] Nonetheless, mainstream science dismisses torsion fields as junk science. In other words, traditional mainstream science has dismissed the existence of scalar wave energy (torsion fields) simply because current measurement tools are based on electromagnetic frequencies, action, and motion, and these measurement tools cannot seem to measure scalar or torsion waves. As we learned from a renowned theoretical physicist, Lisa Randall, earlier, *effective theories are keeping track of measurable details without getting caught in unmeasurable components.* The prevailing scientific paradigm is that that which is not measurable must not be included.

The physics of torsion fields also reveals how language can reprogram our DNA, as previously shared in chapter 6. Russian biophysicist Peter Gariaev and his team have proven the existence of torsion fields. Gariaev's work, wave genetics, utilizes the principles of laser light and sound and scientifically demonstrates that torsion fields carry information to the biophotons of the body, informing the body to heal and grow. Despite the fact that he is healing so-called genetic diseases, the dead-end dogma of prevailing paradigms has yet to accept his progressive research into mainstream avenues.

Truth Is Relative

Moving toward concrescence entails our ability to see truth in all models. Moving toward concrescence will entail our ability to occupy multiple perspectives simultaneously. Concrescence at the collective level begins with concrescence at the individual level.

So are things really falling apart, or are they coming together in a new way?

Everything at the collective level is moving toward integration. The historic split between mind and body has melded. Wave particle duality has been resolved. Science and spirituality are merging, and even separate masculine and feminine constructs are evolving in an integrated, holistic manner. There is an emergence of synthesis.

Synthesis at the individual level is the full recognition and embodiment of our infinite potential with infinite expression; this is a culmination of spirituality with practicality, heart with mind, intuition with logic, limitlessness with limitation. An integration of all aspects of self creates a powerful trajectory for transcending the perceived limitations of duality as reality, to access our full inherent potential. From the boundless state to the fully formed, from illusion to reality, from wave to particle, it is the embracing of the seemingly disparate polarities and the integration of it ALL that propels us forward with a momentum that is unstoppable.

Age of Synthesis

We are living in a time of incredible change, with a chaotic messiness and uncertainty that can feel scary. There are many divergent forces pushing up against each other within systems that are no longer working. Whether we look at political, scientific, medical, religious, cultural, or economic structures, there is a breaking down of what isn't working. At the same time, there is a fusion and blending of parts that does work with other components to create something new.

The artificial boundaries that have historically been drawn to separate mind from matter, spirit from science, and man from technology are softening. Today, many disparate systems are synthesizing. Nothing seems as separate as it did in the past. The boundaries between so-called opposites are beginning to dissolve, and dualities are transforming into an integrated expression of wholeness.

Scientist Dr. Carl W. Hall calls the twenty-first century the Age of Synthesis. According to Hall,

> synthesis is a way of thinking and doing, of providing a vision, in which an idea or a thing, imagined or real, is seen as a coherent whole; often consisting of parts, from which thought can be developed, action can be rejected or taken, and the thing made, assembled, or constructed; either as a new creation or activity or as a duplicate or substitute of known substances.

> The Age of Synthesis is based on the premise that philosophical thought has developed and evolved from the earliest days of learning, undoubtedly preceding written history and usually rooted in the search for truth. For example, early weapons began with the

materials literally at hand, and the desire to improve the capabilities of weapons became a driving force for new methods and materials. Developers responded to "what if . . . ?"—an approach still used, elevating synthesis as an effective approach. As we reflect today and perhaps conclude that the early thinking was primitive, those beginnings were important—each step in the development providing a new foundation for the next step. *Philosophical thought was developed on concepts that became the basis of scientific approaches*, categorized as natural philosophy.[10]

Fluid Boundaries

To bridge the gaps between all paradigms, fostering synthesis and a movement toward concrescence, we are invited to leverage Fluid Boundaries in relation to our models and maps to describe reality and the way we relate to others.

The Integrity Effect includes releasing the fixed boundaries we may have previously established relative to our models and maps, parameters that create a false sense of control over our lives and reality but that also create a real form of limitation and segregation for collective humanity.

Fluid Boundaries are boundaries that aren't predefined in anticipation of situations or experiences. In truth, we never know how a circumstance will present itself before it actually happens. At the quantum level, reality is a series of probabilities that only seem to actualize when we observe them. Fluid Boundaries allow us to move freely among the patterns we encounter in the moment so as to allow for maximal flexibility and flow.

Fluid Boundaries at the interpersonal level are a game-changer. We never know what is going to happen in the very next moment. For example, we never really know how another person is going to show up or respond to us. If boundaries are established in advance, those very boundaries may serve to inform and restrict a situation of circumstance, with the preset limitation triggering a reaction. Thus boundaries can bind us rather than liberate us. Predefined boundaries create separation rather than connection.

For example, we may create boundaries in advance to withstand an expectation of our relative becoming angry with us, and subsequently guilt tripping us up when we tell this person we are taking a vacation to a remote island instead of coming home for the family holidays. The very expectation of the future behavior may indeed be based on prior reactions. Establishing boundaries based on past experiences may actually serve as the trigger for the pattern we were attempting to avoid. This is because an associative reference for the behavior is encoded in the boundary. So instead of avoiding the anger and guilt, the boundary triggers the very pattern we are trying to circumnavigate or avoid.

Conversely, approaching this same anticipated circumstance centered in an open heart, without preconceived notions, with a commitment to notice when circumstances come up as placeholders that may take us out of our hearts, allows for Fluid Boundaries to be created.

When the tendency to move out of the heart occurs, this can serve as a cue to bring in Fluid Boundaries, moving parameters that honor our needs while still allowing others to have their experiences.

Fluid Boundaries without expectations can lead to a softening of the interactions, with others wielding very powerful and often surprising results. It is highly likely that our relative may show understanding, compassion, support, and even a desire to accompany us on the vacation! Whatever the outcome, the possibilities become limitless when navigating with Fluid Boundaries.

Fluid Boundaries Flow with Synthesis

Fluid Boundaries move with flexibility and flow. Sometimes it may seem appropriate, or a matter of habit, to have a fixed boundary. However, this really depends on the pattern with which we are interacting and the complexity of the situation. This is because, when some patterns (or people) encounter a fixed boundary, there is determination to cross it.

Thus Fluid Boundaries can be very useful, because then the pattern or person can't predict where the lines are to cross. It is wise to have a certain amount of dynamic disequilibrium as flow even in the fixed container of boundaries so that we aren't teaching a pattern to be smarter. We do not want to teach a boundary violator how to be more adept at violating boundaries. Fluid Boundaries can allow for us to project and therefore reflect to boundary violators to move back and mind their own state, honoring a shared river of potentials that flows between us.

I approached Melissa several years ago when I felt like I was at a dead end, facing a unique challenge with my son. He was exhibiting a peculiar pattern, finding certain sounds so objectionable that they got him into a fullblown rage, but only when the sounds originated from me. Like any parent, I had questioned myself, blamed myself, examined myself, and after doing the circuit with occupational therapists, music therapists, psychotherapists, and holistic treatments, I was at a point where there seemed to be no clear modalities to pursue and the problem still remained. Yes, there was a name for this syndrome, and if the research and anecdotal evidence were to be believed, it was incurable.

A product of popular parenting advice, my beliefs were that there should be consistency and predictability in raising a child and in enforcing discipline. Every time he exhibited his irrational behavior, I responded with a canned formula. If I was in the car, I would stop the car until he had calmed down, or I would ask him to get out until he was willing to be a responsible passenger; if I was at home, I would react, sometimes with my own rage and need to control. I tried rewards. I tried punishments. I tried pa-

tience and I tried ignoring. Nothing worked, neither for him nor for me.

I asked Melissa to talk to my son, hoping she could some-how "fix" him, but every time I brought this up, she would gently insist that it was I who had reached out to her, I who had made the call, and that if I changed, he would possibly change too. She introduced the concept of Fluid Boundaries.

I came to understand that being consistent and predict-able led only to consistent and predictable outcomes, not to the change and transformation that I was seeking. So far these outcomes had not been productive. I slowly re-alized, through Melissa's guidance, that Fluid Boundaries meant responding to a situation in the moment with full awareness (or as much as I could muster) and that it was not only OK but actually beneficial to respond differently to the same stimulus each time. This was because, as Me-lissa helped me understand, no stimulus was ever exactly the same. Each stimulus was a product of a different time and space, a different mental and emotional state for each person involved in the dynamic. What was important was to be authentic.

Although this may have left my son guessing about my responses, it was not my intention to create insecurity but to create a knowingness that I would come through for him in a way that honored my own state and our com-bined dynamic every single time. Children love to break rules. Unbeknownst to me, I had unconsciously created a child who loved to find a way to defy every firm and rigid boundary that I had set up. When my boundaries started to dissolve and become ever changing, the dynamic be-tween us also became more fluid as we slowly unglued ourselves from our patterns. Many of the unproductive be-haviors on both sides started to dissipate and fade away. It is said, "Change one thing and you change everything." I am happy to report that I saw that adage reflected in my own life. Just applying the concept of Fluid Boundaries had a ripple effect in my relationship with my son, my relationship with my family and friends, and, most significantly, my relationship with myself. In the end, it changed my life. Thank you, Melissa, for meeting me without judgment, right where I was at, and empowering me to liberate myself in the perfect way. —PKD

Fluid Boundaries are also a very useful construct for connecting with others professionally while still honoring our own unique individuality and space.

When I was in massage school, I was taught that I needed to ground, center, and then put up an energetic wall of sorts, so that I wouldn't take on the conditions or negative energy that my clients might be bringing to sessions. This always felt really off to me. Like I was going to battle instead of partnership. It also set up this weird dynamic of somehow being more pure or more positively charged than my client. It didn't allow me the chance to see them as already whole. And this setup carried over into my personal life. I made lots of judgments about whom I needed to shut out energetically and spent a lot of time in protection rituals and reactionary states. And I experienced a ton of dualistic relationships and events as a result.

Fluid Boundaries allow for infinite possibilities and for everyone to show up as their clearest, most neutral, most wholly realized self. They provide honor and acknowledge the safety and power of each person—they provide a space where I can make choices based on what is happening in the moment as opposed to what might have happened before or what I anticipated. Using Fluid Boundaries allows me to focus on myself and what I'm feeling and what I need and be true to that, instead of wasting my time laying energetic bricks in an imaginary wall that does nothing but shut out my ability to see and ensure the sense of isolation and disconnection that I was trying to prevent in the first place. Fluid Boundaries provide options. All of them. —KRS

I am an acupuncturist. In my office when working with clients, I am especially aware of my state. During my intake, I can feel how this already sets the stage for change. When I am in my heart, every acupuncture needle I insert becomes even more so an antenna for universal love and grace. Via resonance, it enables clients to tap into more possibilities for transformation on all levels. I am also able to perceive their situation from other angles and dimensions, that they themselves might not even be aware of or realize. By reflecting what I notice back to them, with Fluid Boundaries, I've seen clients experience some incredible changes in their lives.

The change can sometimes be a most subtle shift in awareness that gives "wiggle room" and opens the door. I had one client who truly believed that if anything could go wrong, it would go wrong for her. She had witnessed this time and time again, thus proving to herself that indeed this is how her life worked. She also pooh-poohed positive thinking, affirmations, and prayer, as those didn't work for her either, and she was pretty much angry at the world for giving her a raw deal. From my heart space, I asked her if she might be able to see how she was reinforcing the same pattern over and over again with her ingrained belief system and thus perpetuating and expecting it. I asked her, "What if there was another way to interact with it?" I saw a glimmer of curiosity in her eye. I proceeded to ask if she was open to going to the "wiggle room" (which made her burst out laughing, something she rarely does), as there she could cut the pattern loose, let go of the duality of good–bad, positive–negative, and just go to the space in between with Fluid Boundaries, where there were many more options available. This offered her a new way of thinking and a sense of freedom that changed up the dynamic. —SG

Fluid Boundaries enable us to let go into the heart, a space of inclusion, without compromising personal integrity. Fluid Boundaries enable us to stand our ground without actually amplifying the very situations or circumstances we may seek to modify. Flexibility of consciousness through Fluid Boundaries is the ability to respond from the field of the heart to what appears to be happening, while effectively navigating through these experiences without losing one's sense of completion, authenticity, joy, and connection to TAS.

Beyond Duality toward Integrating Polarities

Fluid Boundaries enable us to move beyond duality toward integrating polarities. Through Fluid Boundaries, we can recognize that dualized realities split issues so one side cannot see the humanity of the other side. Conversely, polarized sides are still in resonance, as they are interconnected as extensions of unity expressing via a perspective. Polarities often provide a balance for coherence, whereas dualities provide a battle for dominance.

Through Fluid Boundaries, we are able to access the full circumference of possibilities by reconciling perceived opposites within ourselves as well those we come in contact with. Our resonance is not fixed to one singular perspective, nor are we diametrically opposed to anything we encounter.

Fluid Boundaries move us beyond the neutrality of the heart into accelerated gear so we may take actions moving forward that are aligned with the callings of our heart, from a space of inclusion and completion.

From Placeholder to Graceholder

Fluid Boundaries can support us on the path to transcending our placeholders to graceholders. Fluid Boundaries provide freedom through letting go. Letting go, a facet of heart-centered awareness and neutrality, provides an allowance for something new to actualize as a reflection of completion.

There is a difference between letting go with awareness and resistance through resonance. Letting go with awareness is releasing attachment to something needing to change. Resistance through resonance is fighting against something so it will change, dogmatically adhering to an idea, expectation, agenda, model, or belief system that encodes for the way things "should be," "ought to be," or "could be."

Letting go is freedom. Letting go is not giving up. Nor is letting go passive living or an excuse to keep our heads in the sand, ignoring what appears to be happening in our shared realities. Rather, letting go enables us to move beyond the dualistic notions of this way or that way. My way or the highway. Right or wrong. Yours or mine. Letting go is a movement toward inclusion, where either–or becomes AND as possibilities. AND as synthesis. AND as concrescence.

Truth Out

A movement toward concrescence is a movement of integration from a space of completion. Anything that divides, even with revelatory aspects, ultimately disempowers everyone.

There is currently emphasis on revealing "truths" about "lies" perpetuated by a power elite attempting to maintain surrogate control of the masses. At the collective level, consider that any us-versus-them mentality serves to further segregate people.

Many of these "truth-out" organizations (and members) are committed to revealing a deceptive fog that has hovered heavily in our atmosphere, permeating reality with fields of fear, lack, and limitation.

While these people are focused on sharing the so-called truth about these deceptions, they may not realize that any recognition of conspiracy theories revealed from a space of division serves to further segregate consensus reality into dualistic states.

Therefore these truth-out ambassadors actually become conduits of the very powers they are seeking to take down (all the while binging on the dopamine surge fueled by the antagonism). Anything that divides us disempowers all.

This is a very difficult concept for many to understand. So in simplified terms, if we are attempting to bring awareness to a truth from a divisive perspective, that creates a bigger wall between us and them, further perpetuating dualism. The divided focus wins. "We" are still "they" in a house divided.

The gap between sides is perpetuated by the divided focus on the morphic fields of delusion, contortion, and distortion, which will actually gain more power through morphic resonance. The shadows of the illusions become focal points for expression.

When we get our own house in order, uniting the polarities within ourselves, the need to reveal dualistic sides outside ourselves will be replaced with an embodiment of integrated unity within. Embracing the shadows and delusions of confusion from the space of unity and heart-centered awareness will allow for resonant recognition of that which is not truth, but more importantly will attract more truth seekers unto itself.

Even the new age movement that is purportedly committed to waking up the planet may be approaching the awakening from a state of superiority and division between "we who are awake" and "those who slumber." Any time we approach reality with a consciousness of dualism, it will actually create a mitotic environment that continues to further subdivide. Therefore embracing both sides of the polarity, as expressions of one, is the key to opening portals of unity. How many perspectives can we hold in any given moment? The answer is infinite; the one as many.

Superior Supirituality

I define *supirituality* as a superior, (somewhat) smug stance taken by anyone who purports to definitively know what is required for any other person to evolve, transform, and ascend into a "higher" level of spiritual progression.

This includes the trend toward categorizing what is spiritual versus what is not, light worker us-versus-them mentalities, and the excessive use of the term *spiritual bypassing* for any experience that appears not to involve pain, struggle, and many years of concerted effort and time.

We are wise to stop assuming we can ever precisely calibrate another person's movement in consciousness from wherever we "think" we are. We don't know. All we can truly calibrate is our own movement in relation to ourselves. Recognize that spirit as love is imbued in everything. Spirit as love can't be bypassed. Our ideas around spirituality, or science (or the true nature of reality), may only be that . . . our ideas and not absolute truth.

Inclusion removes the extra "u" in *supirituality* and returns it to its free-flowing, integrative, open state. Spirituality. Like love, it is everywhere. Inclusion.

One may feel a false sense of self-importance relative to humanity, a responsibility to shed light on these cabals of darkness and movements that seek to disempower many to potentially save the controlling few. It is important to consider that this is potentially an enlightenment trap. Any sense of superiority or any sense of being higher or better than anyone or anything is not an act of spirit. One must remember that spirit is imbued in all, and that everything is the nothing expressing itself, and that even the darkest patterns contain within them seeds of light as love's completion. Holding those patterns in a space of loving grace from the field of the heart supports possible movement and recognition that they, too, are light.

The Integrity Effect integrates us versus them into you and me in the shared WE experience.

PRACTICAL PLAY

Consider a challenging situation or circumstance either at home, at work, or in a prevailing paradigm where dualism and us-versus-them mentalities typically prevail. This may be a political, medical, economic, or even environmental concern that has created divisiveness.

Write this challenge down if you choose. Also write down any thoughts, feelings, sensations, or experiences that occur for you as you consider this problem from your point of view.

Center in the field of the heart or in your Love-sphere (refer to chapter 4 for assistance).

From the heart-field, reconsider this challenge of opposing viewpoints from the holo-frame of a placeholder. What thoughts, feelings, sensations, or experiences occur for you now in relation to this placeholder that is your viewpoint? Write this down if you choose.

Now consider the opposing view as a placeholder. What thoughts, feelings, sensations, or experiences occur for you as you connect to the alternate perspective? If you are having difficulty with this, you may want to integrate the placeholder into your heart. From this space of synthesis, write down anything that occurs for you.

Now, with the integration and synthesis of both or many sides of this challenge, how will this opportunity as a placeholder influence your choices moving forward? In other words, what choices will you make differently? What actions will you take? How does this Practical Play assist you in leveraging Fluid Boundaries?

For example:

Recently I was very frustrated by the political election in America. It seemed almost everyone was divided. For a little while, I found myself immersed in the division, choosing sides based on the limited information I had in any given moment (real news,

*fake news). I felt divided within myself, and as a re-
sult, I felt angry, disempowered, and afraid of what
might happen, depending on which of the candidates
was elected.*

*Then I dropped into the field of my heart and con-
sidered the election from the framework of a placeholder. I looked at both sides of the political divide
from the field of the heart. I integrated the placeholder of divided political views into my heart and
was able to see many relative truths and possibilities
from multiple sides.*

*Multiple recognitions surfaced when looking at
this overall pattern as a placeholder. I realized I am
neither for nor against any political candidate or political party. I am neither for nor against real news or
fake news. I realized I am for raising the consciousness of the planet, and this means ending the great
divide within ourselves. I saw clearly that I know the
difference between sharing information to increase
awareness and sharing information to perpetuate
divisiveness. This is an important distinction that
can be clarifying for anyone when weeding through
the plethora of information we are bombarded with
daily.*

*The consciousness we hold when we are sharing
information (and receiving information) is as important as the information we may be resonating with.
I saw from my heart with respect to the latest political election that perhaps the most expedited route to
wake individuals out of apathy and indifference was
going to unfold. The pockets of division, discrimina-
tion, bigotry, and inequality that have been cloaked
in political rhetoric may be coming to the surface to
clear. Our filters are lifting. One nation divided is
still one nation. One world divided is still one world.*

*From a horizontal perspective, this can feel scary,
but from a vertical, holonomic perspective, it is ab-*

solutely awesome. I chose to look both vertically and horizontally at all patterns, for where the two merge at the zero point is the nexus of truth. There is zero point in choosing sides, for all sides are still inherently connected. My heart said, "Choose your truth wisely."

I saw from my heart that no political candidate can save us from ourselves. As a result of this Practical Play, I decided it was time to get involved with groups who were feeling very scared about the future based on pending political reconfigurations. I would assist them to be the change we want to see in our candidates, in our paradigms, and in humanity overall. I would assist them with synthesis and concrescence.

The Integrity Effect can help us to reclaim our power by no longer projecting our division out into the collective consciousness of humanity. Thank you for looking deep within your heart to discover that you know the truth already . . . and that all the noise, fear, and uncertainty are simply attractions to distraction.

We can change existing paradigms not by fighting them but by curiously interacting with them from the field of the heart and by letting go. We can leverage Fluid Boundaries to move from a predefined past to the realm of infinite possibility, through the heart of completion. Let go into the heart of completion. Allow for synthesis and notice as soon as now that concrescence has occurred.

That which has integrity is sustainable. As we move forward from our hearts to experience the Integrity Effect, we are reminded that we have nothing before us, and so we have everything before us. The shorelines of our new reality await our new collective heart-prints.

The future rests peacefully in the chamber of our eternal hearts. Now is the time to step into the Integrity Effect. One is enough. You are enough. You are the completion. We are the completion. How will we choose to Play?

11

Distinctions, Curiosity, and Living into the Answer

Be curious and try to find solutions to problems.

—Lisa Randall, theoretical physicist

Life is connection. We are all intricately and inexorably connected to everything. How we notice this connection is what transcends the seemingly mundane to the extraordinary.

If we could love others' differences as much as we love our shared similarities, we would live in a different world. It only takes a moment to appreciate our diversity as much as our similarities. What would it be like if . . . ? Open into the answer from the field of the heart. It only takes a moment to curiously live into the answer.

It is perhaps unusual to write the final chapter of a book before a book has been written. Yet this is what is occurring, for in all endings are new beginnings. What we deem the end is simply a moment in time, isolated from the whole of eternity in which content and context are created.

How can I write the conclusion of this book when I don't even know what has been written? There really is no particular order in which we are supposed to do things, from start to finish. There is no linear progression for the creative process and for creating new heart-prints. Perhaps it is done before it has begun. All ideas, all creative impulses, contain within them the seeds of love's completion.

Second Guess

A second is defined as 9,192,631,770 vibrations of a cesium atom at a specified state of electronic excitement, no matter how long that takes.

Two weeks; 14 days; 336 hours; 20,160 minutes; 1,209,600 seconds. Successive moments of now woven together, no matter how long that takes.

Two weeks was the increment of time that I scheduled to be at my writing sanctuary in Cabo San Lucas, Mexico, to work on this book. It was Christmas break, and while most people were opening presents and frolicking with family and friends, I had made a commitment to myself to get this book written . . . or mostly written. After all, I wrote the first three books in the same manner, between teaching seminars while on holiday breaks. I knew what to expect and exactly how to make it happen. I would be 100 percent focused and fully immersed in the writing process.

Or so I thought.

Admittedly, somehow this year's trip felt different. As I packed my bag the night before my flight, I sensed this journey would change me beyond the transformations I inevitably experienced in the sole process of writing, receiving, and opening to new information. "Writing always changes me," my mind reasoned, to which my heart replied, "Yes, and this time will be different."

As I looked upon my bookshelf for the reference books I would need to support my writing process, my eyes landed on a nonfiction book titled *Wild* by Cheryl Strayed. It was a story of a young woman who hiked the Pacific Northwest Trail solo for three months following her mother's death and her own divorce. I had not yet read the book, although strangely enough it had accompanied me twice previously to Mexico while I wrote.

I contemplated bringing the book again and immediately had a flash of thought of a woman I had sat next to at the beach the prior year while writing. She had mentioned her mother had passed when she was very young. I sensed this *Wild* book would be meaningful to her. For whatever reason, I packed the book. It needed to come even if I did not read it. I packed several other books and the minimal attire I needed while being an ocean scribe.

The day following my flight, I arrived at my writing sanctuary with my iPhone, all ready to write. I have an abnormal process in that I write my books entirely on my iPhone under an umbrella to the sound of the ocean waves. Upon arrival my first evening, I went to bed at a decent hour so I could get an early-morning start on the manuscript. However, when I woke up the next day, I noticed that my bedside table was covered with water. It seemed the cup of water I had poured before bed had a crack in its base and had slowly leaked water onto the table throughout the night. This leak drenched everything on the surface of the table, including my iPhone.

Within minutes, my iPhone shut down and would not power up, no matter what I tried to do. I panicked. What if my phone was permanently damaged and I was unable to write the book with the same flow as my last few books? Although I had another electronic device with me on the trip, I was most efficient on my phone, as the gadget was essentially an extension of me. My fingers move at astronomical speed on the virtual keyboard. My phone was my comfort zone for writing, and writing was my purpose for being there, away from family and friends and the usual "distractions" of everyday life. I was very concerned, and yet I heard my heart speak clearly: "Trust all is in order." And so I did. I chose to trust.

Resolved to still "be productive," I grabbed a few books on hyperdimensional physics from my bag and also the copy of *Wild* (just for fun) and headed down to stake my corner of ocean paradise. As I walked past the people lounging in the sun, I noticed a familiar couple sleeping in a covered hammock. I recognized them from the previous year but had never spoken to them. I wondered for a moment what their story was.

I approached my favorite spot in the corner of the resort and saw the woman I had spoken to the year before (whose mother had died when she was young), whom I had thought of while packing for the trip, as well as her friend. They were sitting in my spot. So I chose the next best option and sat down in the lounge chair next to them.

Out came my reading materials. Time to get serious. I reasoned to myself that if I could not write, it was because I need to study more, in order to glean additional understanding not yet articulated in my prior books. I opened to chapter 1 in a book about exploring extra dimensions of space and time and began to read.

My concentration was interrupted as a result of the chattering of the women sitting next to me. For some strange reason, rather than being mildly irritated, as I normally would have been when trying to work, I found their conversation soothing. They weren't talking about anything in particular. But their communication carried such ease, comfort, and humor that it was pleasant to be around. Clearly these two women had a strong bond, a connection between them that was palpable. Being near them felt good. Harmonious. Playful. Fun.

I had remembered meeting them both briefly the prior year. Apparently these women had been watching me for a few years writing my books on my iPhone. They had developed all sorts of theories about what I was doing. Why was I alone? Who was I texting? Was I taking selfies or reading on the tiny device? How on earth could my fingers move so fast? When we first spoke last year, I had told them I was writing a book and briefly explained what it was about. In exchange, they told me what they did for a living, where they resided, and a little bit about themselves. On the surface, we seemed to have little in common other than our shared love for this particular ocean get-away.

As I sat reading my book near these women, trying to decipher phase conjugation of standing waves and the practical value of becoming a living laser, I looked out beyond my book to see what the woman whose mother had died was reading. I was astonished as she held within her hands the book *Wild*, the very book that had triggered me to think of her while I packed my bag.

Synchronicity: A Meaningful Coincidence and Cue to Pay Attention

A few moments later, a new couple approached the women and greeted them with hugs and high fives. They had just arrived from the airport and were waiting for their room to be ready. They all seemed delighted to see each other. I overheard that the couple had gone to another resort last Christmas and so it had been two years since they had all seen each other. Soon thereafter, the couple from the hammock approached. They seemed to know the new arrivals, and again there were hugs and high fives. I half listened as people spoke of what they had been doing since last time they saw one another. A year had passed for some. Two years had passed for others. And yet there was a meeting in the moment that seemed to transcend time.

For the next ten days, I didn't write a word. My iPhone never recovered, and while my mind wanted to worry, my heart was full of delight with the unexpected camaraderie of this newly formed group of us who had come together. Within that small increment of time, I experienced such heartfelt connection, camaraderie, affection, true authentic acceptance, and genuine joy that it is hard to fathom this trip unfolding any other way.

We all had vastly different backgrounds, careers, and even nationalities. Our stories were as diverse as our preferences and perspectives. Yet there was an appreciation for our differences as much as our similarities. We were lawyers, teachers, psychologists, analysts, engineers, builders, entrepreneurs, administrators, and domestic managers (housewives and househusbands), and yet we were all so much more. We were all so much more than our jobs or our various stories.

We experienced a convergence, unplanned and yet perhaps destined in some sense. Our hearts were open, and together we created new heart-prints.

And Then There Was One

The last of the crew left at the tail end of my trip. We were sad but felt complete when it was time to go. I would be the only one remaining for a few days of quiet time. "See you next December," we all said to each other with some uncertainty. Who knows where any of us will be a year from now? We could plan for another meet-up, but what if life leads us all in different directions?

That final morning, from afar, I saw two of my friends departing for the airport. They did not see me. We had said many good-byes already, so I thought it was best to just let them go without further adieus. A second after their car departed, a few of the others appeared looking for them to say good-bye again. They had missed each other by only a moment. It seemed our paths were slightly out of alignment that day as we returned to our separate universes. Our trajectories were moving in different directions.

I smiled to myself as I realized how many forces seemingly conspired to bring us together. The multitude of synchronicities that occurred while we were a group, and then how the universe gently pulled us apart when it was time to go. How beautiful. We did not need to say a final good-bye. We would perhaps meet again next year, a moment in time when all our diverging paths would come together again on the same plane of location, one meeting point. Unity. Concrescence; the growing together and merging of like or unlike separate parts or particles.

Where might we all be a year from now? I pondered. *Where would I be a year from now?* I wondered, and then as soon as now, I let it go. I knew I could be anywhere I chose. And with that realization, I looked up at the horizon, at the brilliant sea of limitless waves of potential in front of me. In joy, I open my tattered copy of *Wild* and began to read. I could still hear the sounds of my new dear friends in the background as though they were present. Cackles, mumbles, insights, teasing, shared silence at sunrise and sunset. I could see them in my mind's eye, looking at me with loving smiles as though we had known each other for years. They had found a place in my heart and healed a part of me I did not know needed healing.

I missed them, and yet I knew that for the next few days I was meant to be alone, to write and reflect upon the bonds that were created while we were together and to consider the relevance of this experience to living the Integrity Effect. *I hope I can capture it all,* I thought to myself. And as quickly as I had that thought, I heard my heart say, "Nothing to capture. Simply flow. Every moment is complete just like you are. So stay present to the now, and what you seek to express will move through you in perfect synchrony. Choose to flow."

Just Look Up

It has been exactly one year since the moment I looked up from my phone and opened my heart to new friends and new distinctions. What a difference a year makes. I am back in Mexico writing the final chapters of *The Integrity Effect*, with the exception of this chapter. This one was (mostly) already written.

The gang is here again minus one, and we picked up a new member too. We have come together as community, with our different perspectives, in the same ease and grace that brought us together last year. For a passage of time, these people and I will be together as a cohesive WE, while

I move in and out of the group to write to my heart's content.

Santa has just arrived on the beach by horseback, and in the background I hear a vacationer in a hot tub singing holiday carols loudly and very off tune: "Do you see what I see? Do you hear what I hear?" I smile at yet another synchrony that perhaps only a wholly orchestrated universe could deliver.

No one sees what you see. No one hears what you hear. You are unique. Your perspective is yours and yours alone; it is part of what makes you special, but your perspective does not define you. Perspective, like story, simply enables us to make distinctions and to learn through contrast. Perspectives change as we change our filters. We can change the way we look at ourselves, the way we talk to ourselves, and the way we treat ourselves. We can change how we feel about ourselves. We can change how we relate to ourselves, and therefore we can change how we relate to everything.

How we choose to live now and in the very next moment can change. Our hearts know we are more than our perspectives and feelings combined. Our hearts know we are all love.

We can live that knowingness, and with curiosity, we can choose to live in to the answer.

It's been a difficult year for most everyone in the group, perhaps for most people everywhere. Yet despite our challenges, we have all made new distinctions, and we are all still here, breathing in possibilities and exhaling experience. Indeed, this past year has been filled with many opportunities, characterized by excessive contrast and successive choice points.

For me, most of the year was focused on fully integrating and testing the physics of the Integrity Effect in every compartment of my life—in relation to myself, friends, family, work, in the community, and with the world at large.

This is not unlike my days in the pharmaceutical industry when preparing to launch a new drug. After memorizing the package insert for all the drug indications and side effects, I would always try each drug on myself before presenting samples to physicians. I wanted to personally experience each medication before convincing doctors to prescribe the drugs to patients. Some might say this "sampling of the goods" was dangerous or not very smart. In hindsight, I somewhat agree, and yet I wanted to know from personal experience what I was advocating to others.

Prescription for Integrity

And so, while I have been teaching the principles of the Integrity Effect for several years, I wanted to prescribe my own medicine wherever integrity may have been lacking. In the past year, I chose to dive all in and fully immerse myself more cohesively with the principles shared throughout this book.

I asked for anything in my life that was not fully in integrity to reveal itself to me. I asked some open-ended questions: *What would my life look like if every aspect of my life reflected the Integrity Effect? How might my life transform in the next year if anything out of alignment were to be revealed? What changes would occur for me? What would dissolve and what would evolve accordingly?* Then I observed with curiosity all that was unfolding around me. Some parts of my life appeared to be falling apart, and as I watched through the eyes of integrity, I could indeed see that things were coming together in new, more empowering ways.

Since asking that question and living into the answer, I have taken the Integrity Effect to a whole new level, or perhaps integrity has taken me to a whole new level. It is amazing what can happen when we make a commitment to fully love ourselves, as we choose to live in and live out the principles of the Integrity Effect. It is as though the universe says thank you in exponential fashion.

With coherency and congruency, in the past year, I have continued to let go of so much that was not aligned with my heart. I released many relationships that were not aligned with integrity. At the same time, I strengthened bonds with those who genuinely loved me. I made new friends and colleagues who didn't manipulate or try to use me. I rekindled relationships with some estranged relatives and redefined the way other family members would need to treat me if they wanted to share in my life.

I stopped supporting structures and groups that were not supporting me. At work, I completely changed how I did things, reconfiguring business contracts and partnerships in a manner that is equal service to self and equal service to others. I said yes to opportunities that previously I would have cowered from in fear.

The Ricochet Effect was reduced to a minimum across all aspects of my life. On the rare occasion when the ricochet has occurred, the rebound and recovery have been almost instantaneous. Many placeholders transformed into graceholders.

This has been a year of distinctions and deliberately choosing to fully love, honor, and commit to heart-centered awareness, TAS, and the power-packed potential of the Integrity Effect. Am I 100 percent in integrity? I do not know the answer definitively. Is anyone ever fully in integrity? The answer varies on a moment-by-moment basis, one heart-print at a time. The Integrity Effect is not a goal to be reached, when all placeholders become graceholders. There is no grade to be assigned or percentage to be allocated. Rather, the Integrity Effect is a grace to be received, gifted as wholeness.

I know I am a work (play) in progress, doing the best that I can in every moment to trust my heart and choose accordingly. That's all any of us can do. And that is enough. I am enough. You are enough. We are enough. Do I stumble? Indeed. And I get up again as quickly as I fall. Will you stumble? Perhaps. It's totally OK. The Integrity Effect is not a path of perfection. The Integrity Effect is a path of perfect-imperfection, where self-love trumps judgment and authenticity overrides expectations.

A sincere willingness to show up for ourselves with curiosity and a desire to play with the principles of the Integrity Effect can change everything from the inside out. Ask yourself, "What would my life look like if I genuinely loved myself?" "How might what I have learned throughout the pages of this book change my experiences in the next year, in the next month, in the very next moment?"

> My experience of the M-Joy teachings have been a playful interaction with myself and the environment around me. My relationship with the world has changed from the inside out. I find myself calmer and responding to life's challenges, rather than living in emotional reaction. My self-expression is clearer and more neutral. I now feel a sense of oneness with my everyday experiences. Certainly I'm more loving, peaceful, and happy. —KM

Now is the time to live into the answer. We can recognize the value of distinctions occurring along an endless continuum of love at the personal and collective levels. Our challenges are placeholders as opportunities, and our perceived limitations are springboards for personal and collective evolution.

How do we fully experience a movement from placeholder to graceholder? We can't pretend. It happens when it happens, no matter how long that takes. This movement can happen in a moment . . . or through the continuity of time. The movement from placeholder to graceholder happens when we truly, authentically let go. We let go of our rigid notions and old emotions. We release our horizontal filters that come in multiple shades of separation and adorn new filters made of love's vertical completion.

Everything may indeed be love at its core essence—and yet there are distinct expressions of interwoven contrast that may appear to be anything other than . . . love. So how do we find coherent love in all that appears otherwise? How do we recognize love in the plethora of circumstances that seem to reflect fear, separation, alienation, oppression, and sorrow? What is the value of these distinctions in our awareness?

All is love . . . and distinctions.

The value of distinctions is that they provide us with reflections (as distortions) for what we may not really want, enabling us to get clear on what we really do want. Thus we are able to leverage the contrast to choose what we are willing (or not willing) to show up for and experience. Contrast provides us with clarity, a mirror and window into choice with discernment from the field of the heart.

Curiosity about contrast offers us the ability to move away from what is not self-loving, into the gap of what is yet to come in wholeness. Our placeholders evolve into graceholders when we let go and live into the answer.

Curiosity Cures Us

I have often contemplated whether the true lesson to learn is that we don't have to do anything the hard way, through forgetting, contrast, and suffering. We don't have to do it any which way. We get to choose how to do it, if only we realize this.

There is no judgment in learning any lesson through trial and tribulation. And it is not necessarily the only way. My greatest growth has sometimes come from the darkest spaces within myself, reflected by shadowed circumstances without, and in feeling broken.

Yet the light was never absent. My wholeness was always intact. Rather, I had merely moved in my awareness away from this recognition, distancing self from self. Deceptions of perceptions.

Lessons can be immediate in the acceptance of our true essence. Let go into easy. Let go into curiosity.

Be a perpetually curious adventurer in all aspects of life. Curiosity flows us fully into the Integrity Effect in our endeavors, with childlike wonder. Curiosity is the velocity of love's infinite potential that emerges from our hearts. Curiosity *opens* us, and when we are open, more becomes available, probable, and therefore likely to actualize. Curiosity enables us to live into the answer.

What would it be like if . . . anything is possible?

How might we live into that answer now?

What would it be like if we were to see reality through the delighted eyes of a child holding a puppy for the very first time?

What would happen if we were to trust the universe, trust ourselves, and trust our hearts to support us, nurture us, and love us?

How might letting go into our hearts liberate us now?

How might living into the answer with curiosity, delight, and wonder change the way we create and relate to everything?

All is love . . . and distinctions of all that appears otherwise. Make choices aligned with the symmetry of heart-centered awareness. Consistent heart-centered choices create the template for a new reality where every moment is a miracle.

What would it be like now if . . . ?

Live into the answer.

Love into the answer.

Open-ended questions provide for a natural movement in awareness from where we are now to where we want to be. Experience curiosity as a powerful, transformative way of relating. The question is the answer, and that answer rests within our hearts, awaiting recognition. Curiosity cultivates new maps for unity, love, and connection amid contrast and distinctions. Connect to curiosity.

This is not the end. This is the beginning. This is the middle. This is completion. Now. We have everything before us and nothing before us. How we choose to navigate from here is entirely our choice. Our hearts know exactly what to do to create new maps and new distinctions. Connect to the heart of it all and map the experience of the Integrity Effect.

Go forth with curiosity and create new heart-prints one choice at a time. Just choose.

In-Joy!

Melissa Joy

Glossary (and Mel-isms)

Abductive logic. A form of logic that starts with an incomplete set of observations and proceeds to the likeliest possible conclusion.

Abundance. A state of consciousness. A currency of infinite potential, expressing as flow. Abundance is a state of being or resonant vibration that lacks nothing. Resonate with abundance, and abundance flows into all that you are and all that you do. The essence of abundance is the recognition that all is available.

Acceptance. Allowance for *what is,* through neutrality, to facilitate change. Letting go of resistance to anything.

Addiction. A placeholder in awareness that represents an attempt to find True Authentic Self (TAS) and simultaneously avoid it. The placeholder that the addiction pattern represents serves as a habituated strategy to avoid recognizing self as an infinitely whole, perfect, and limitless being having an experience of limitation. The pattern as placeholder serves as a habituated strategy to look for fulfillment and acceptance of TAS in something outside of self that is inherently and incessantly empty. In this recognition, there is freedom to recondition awareness and embrace integrity. There is freedom to move from dis-ease to flow in total acceptance, to choose anew. Just choose.

All. Everything in totality. All is impersonal in nature and extends far beyond individual awareness, beyond the fabric of space-time, and beyond anything we may think we know definitively. Universal consciousness is all. In its entirety, it is void of perspective and identity because it includes all vantage points as part of itself. All is Love, and Love is all. (*See also* Universal consciousness)

Allowance. A state of acceptance that provides for a natural letting go of any negative charge that keeps our perspective on our reality locked into the polarity and duality of what we are attempting to discharge or transcend. In other words, a state of acceptance and allowance releases the unwanted charge against anything. (*See also* Acceptance)

Association memes. Memes that have been conceptually fused in our awareness. They are a bit like attitudes, because the presence of one meme triggers a thought or an emotion or another meme.

Biophotons. Light emissions. It has been scientifically proven that every cell in the body emits more than one hundred thousand light impulses or photons per second. These light emissions, found in all living things, have been found to be the driving mechanism behind all biochemical reactions.

Caudate nucleus. Integrates complex emotions and thoughts about love. The caudate nucleus (CAU) is all about making choices, but it is also connected to addictions because of its role in feeling pleasure, relief, and comfort. Produces the neuro-transmitter dopamine. The caudate nucleus lies in the middle of the head and looks a bit like a medium-sized shrimp—two shrimp, actually, as each hemisphere of the brain has its own caudate. The caudate and other regions of the striatum have connections to the cerebral cortex, the top, multifolded layer of the brain with which we do our thinking. It has connections, too, with memory areas and with the ventral tegmental area (VTA).

Change. To make or become different. Change is a constant. The nature of change is flow. Change happens naturally when we are no longer resistant to *what is* and when we are no longer pushing against something or someone in an attempt to create transformation. (*See also* Transform)

Choice. Our inherent ability to choose where to resonate in our awareness. The power of choice creates the rhythm of our individual and collective realities. Our choices determine our experiences.

Choice with discernment. Making choices aligned with our heart that reflect our personal integrity. We have more options and we make better decisions.

Choose. The process of aligning awareness with a possibility state to establish resonance so that a possibility becomes a probability that expresses as experience. Just choose.

Choose, notice, let go, allow, trust, choose anew. A method for experiencing change. *Choose* a pattern that you want to change or manifest. Drop down into the field of the heart and *notice* the connection. *Let go* and release all attachment and resistance to change. Let go into neutrality. *Allow* the pattern you noticed to exist in your awareness as a placeholder while also noticing the presence of other possibilities. *Trust* what you notice. *Choose anew* where you want to resonate. Choose In-Joy.

Coherence. A unified field of undifferentiated consciousness potential that has not been defined or formed; also used to describe an unbroken connection with universal consciousness. For example, when we are in heart-centered awareness, we are easily able to access a state of coherence with universal consciousness, which may be observed by feelings of joy, connectivity, and synchronicity. Coherence is a reflection of our universal connection as flow. In physics, it is a correlation between the phases of two or more waves so that interference effects may be produced between them. Also, coherence is a correlation between the phases of parts of a single wave.

Coherency, congruency, and integrity in action. I define the *coherency* of True Authentic Self (TAS) as awareness of an unbroken connection to one's true essence as limitless potential expressed as flow. *Congruency* is alignment of awareness of this coherent connection with everything *in relation to,* or relating to, self. *Integrity* is the expression of coherency and congruency in all intentions and actions.

Collateral damage. Injury inflicted on something other than an intended target. It has been my experience that when relating to others, if we do not establish boundaries of what we are willing to show up for when others are not in integrity, we experience the Ricochet Effect and become collateral damage.

Collective consciousness. The condition of the individual within the whole of society and how any given individual comes to view himself or herself as a part of any given group. Specifically, the term has been used by social theorists/psychoanalysts like Durkheim, Althusser, and Jung to explain how an autonomous individual comes to identify with a larger group/structure. Definitively, *collective* means "formed by a collection of individual persons or things; constituting a collection; gathered into one; taken as a whole; aggregate, collected." *Consciousness* is more complex and harder to define in all its implications. *The Oxford English Dictionary* defines it as "joint or mutual knowledge; internal knowledge or conviction; knowledge as to which one has the testimony within oneself, esp. of one's own innocence, guilt, deficiencies," and as "the state or fact of being mentally conscious or aware of anything." By combining the two terms, we can surmise that the phrase *collective consciousness* implies internal knowledge or a consciousness shared by a plurality of persons. The easiest way to think of collective consciousness, even with its extremely loaded historical content, is to regard it as being an idea or proclivity that we all share.

Compartmentalization (*also* compartmentalize *or* come-apart-mental-lies). Segregation and delineation of aspects of our awareness, producing a lack of integration, synchronization, harmony, and flow in our life. Compartmentalization of our spiritual journey occurs when anything we consider *spiritual* is siphoned off from other various facets of our experienced reality. Any delineation made between spiritual and practical or between spiritual and physical, mental, emotional, relational, or financial—are somewhat arbitrary. Such delineations become true when we resonate with them as if they were separate categories of consciousness. In a sense, all categories or compartments are memes, most of which have corresponding global morphic fields. Because spirit is infused in everything, compartmentalizing spirit essentially means segregating that which is the all from itself. Yet, it is not possible to compartmentalize spirit. Spirit is not about anything, as it is everything *and* nothing. We can only compartmentalize our ideas about spirit. Consciousness as spirit, source, nature, field, love, light, or whatever we want to call it, does not discriminate. Spirit includes everything, including duality with its seemingly discrete polarities. Spirit, consciousness—whatever you call it—just *is*. When we cease to compartmentalize, then "come apart the mental lies" we have told ourselves about our limitations versus what is infinitely possible. Spirit has no limits, and neither do we.

Compassion and completion. Found within True Authentic Self (TAS), a combined state of being that transcends the perceived need for comparison and competition with others. When we show ourselves compassion, and honor the completion that is inherently within us all, then we are no longer driven to project our sense of lack onto others; we no longer compare and compete to feel worthy. In this recognition of our TAS, we end the self-betrayal and befriend the world.

Compassionate empathy. Entraining our resonant vibration to our heart-fields, which expresses through us as love and coherent light, and then aligning awareness to another's resonance. This enables us to mind our state without entraining to another's disposition.

Concrescence. The coalescence or growing together of parts originally separate. The concept of concrescence originated in biology and was later adopted by philosopher Alfred North Whitehead in his book *Process and Reality* as part of a philosophical ontology.

Congruence. Alignment of the awareness of our coherent connection with everything that relates to self.

Consciousness. Per *Merriam-Webster's Dictionary,* "the quality or state of being aware, especially of something within oneself; the state or fact of being conscious of an external object, state, or fact." Therefore, that which is conscious has perspective when observing what it perceives. As defined in this book, consciousness includes everything and excludes nothing. It does not stem from the universe, but instead, it is understood here that the universe stems from consciousness. Consciousness is all. (*See also* Universal consciousness)

Consciousness potential. As used in this book, consciousness potential is *no-thing* because it has not yet expressed itself as something. Consciousness potential is universal consciousness *before* consciousness creates, actualizes, and/or experiences. Consciousness potential is void of distinctions or boundaries, and therefore, it also has no limitations. Undifferentiated consciousness potential is limitless, formless, weightless, timeless, without space, without thought, and totally free. Consciousness potential is unconditional love before love expresses through conditions.

Constructs. Configurations of information contained or held in a specific form. Examples of constructs of consciousness include, but are not limited to, ideas, opinions, and beliefs.

Containers. Constructs of information that gives shape and form to an experience. Examples of containers are morphic fields, memes, masks, and personas.

Contrast. A calibration through which light, as awareness, notices its own movement. Through this awareness, light grows into more light, shining bright for the benefit of all. We can learn the most about our own light, vibration, and potential through contrast. Contrast allows for the cultivation of awareness between two states: the inertia and stagnation of perceived darkness (light distanced from itself) and the momentum and expansion of light as love. As we perceive the contrast, light is actually able to launch its momentum further. In other words, the more light we shine into the shadows or darkness we perceive, the less the shadows or darkness affect us. By perceiving the contrast, we gain awareness and awaken to our True Authentic Self and to the TAS of others, too. Remember, shadows and darkness are light distanced in awareness from itself. Shining light offers a form of remembering and a beacon for self and others to return to the light as the love we truly are. Contrast can serve as leverage, not as a hindrance. Contrast can propel curiosity, creativity, and conscious awareness, and thus it serves as a springboard for change.

Current configuration of conscious expression. Current reality constructs; our current state of being; our experience of ourselves as we presently perceive *the way things are*. Our configuration can be either rigid, where things do not appear to change, or in flow, where change happens naturally.

Deductive logic. If something is true of a class of members in general, it is also true for all members of that class.

Desires. Inner sensations of curiosity that propel us to take action in a certain direction. When listened to, True Authentic Desires (TAD) that well up from the field of the heart spark a creative impulse that leads us to experience the unfolding of our true magnificence. (*See also* True Authentic Desires)

Disease (dis-ease). A state of being that describes a lack of ease and flow within the interconnected systems of the individual body hologram. In this state of being, symptoms of disease are often clustered together and labeled as a diagnosis. Classified in terms of diagnoses, diseases are engineered morphic fields. (*See also* Wellness)

Distinction memes. Arbitrary delineations made by labeling and categorizing reality.

Done. At a transformative level, *done* refers to the state in which the patterns we were entangled with that prevented us from loving unconditionally have been released. Done does not necessarily mean we are done interacting with a pattern altogether. There are many levels of done and each offer us a different prism of awareness.

Ego. A powerful tool for expression when it follows as an extension of the heart. Our True Authentic Self (TAS) invites us to accept ego and invites ego to follow as the heart leads us into manifesting the desires that consciousness is continually creating. In all endeavors, our TAS first lives from the heart and then integrates ego as a useful expression and interface with reality. When we embrace ego as an extension of us, as a placeholder in awareness, ego simply *is* as a part of our continual unfolding. When we perceive ego as something to destroy or control, then the idea of ego is still seeking to destroy itself. The more we battle ego, the more we are enslaved by the idea of ego. Constructs can constrict us. But, when constructs are integrated, they can liberate us.

Electromagnetic field of the heart. According to research conducted at HeartMath Institute: "The heart generates the body's most powerful and most extensive rhythmic electromagnetic field. Compared to the electromagnetic field produced by the brain, the electrical component of the heart's field is about sixty times greater in amplitude and permeates every cell in the body. The magnetic component is approximately five thousand times stronger than the brain's magnetic field and can be detected several feet away from the body using sensitive magnetometers."

Elevator process (E-love-ator). Process for dropping into the field of the heart. Visualize an elevator. See a miniature version of yourself stepping into the elevator and allow the doors to close. Press the Down button. Follow your awareness as the elevator descends out of your head, down through your throat, and even further down into your chest cavity. Allow the elevator doors to open. What do you notice?

Emotional intelligence (EQ or EI). A term created by two researchers, Peter Salavoy and John Mayer, and popularized by Dan Goleman in his 1996 book of the same name. Emotional intelligence is the ability to identify and manage your own emotions and the emotions of others.

Empathy. As defined by *Merriam-Webster's*, "Understanding, being aware of, being sensitive to, and experiencing the feelings, thoughts, and experience of another of either the past or present without having the feelings, thoughts, and experience fully communicated in an objective manner"; also, the capacity for this.

Energy. We do not know what energy is. We know what energy does. Energy is defined in the dictionary as the ability or capacity to do work.

Explanation. A set of statements that make something clear or easy to understand. Also, the act or process of telling, showing, or being the reason for or cause of something. Any explanation uses language to articulate something that language cannot adequately explain. Explanations are simply bridges for our individual awareness to comprehend something that transcends explanation. Words as carrier waves convey what we perceive might be happening, not what is *actually* happening. We can never know with absolute certainty what is *actually* happening. The moment we decide that we know with certainty what is happening, we actually limit what we can access. Remember, concepts and explanations serve as maps to describe the territory of consciousness, but they are not the territory itself.

Exponents of grace. When coupled with components of grace, a component of the field of the heart can be amplified or multiplied. This component of the heart-field can be expressed as a mathematical equation for accessing personal power wherein the Heart-Field × Grace = Exponential Personal Power (HF × G = EPP). As with any mathematical equation, the components of grace can extend in multiple directions. Any component of personal power, when divided by grace, can summate and consummate the various functions of the field of the heart. They are interrelated, interconnected, interdependent, symbiotic, synergistic, synchronistic, tessared, and torsioned.

FanTAStic. The experience of discovering, embodying and experiencing True Authentic Self (TAS). This experience is also noticed in True Authentic Relating (TAR) and when manifesting True Authentic Desires (TAD). Experiencing fanTAStic is not fantasy. It is a joyful new reality of you *in relation to* . . . everything!

Fear. Love in a confused state.

Field of the heart. The field of the heart provides us with direct access to our inner voice, our inner wisdom, and our inner chamber of limitless potential. (*See* Heartfield)

Fluid Boundaries. Fluid Boundaries are boundaries that aren't predefined in anticipation of situations or experiences. In truth, we never know how a circumstance will present itself before it actually happens. At the quantum level, reality is a series of probabilities that only seem to actualize when we observe them. Fluid Boundaries allow us to move freely among the patterns we encounter in the moment so as to allow for maximal flexibility and flow. Fluid Boundaries foster synthesis and concrescence.

Fractal. A self-similar structure that remains the same regardless of the scale to which it is enlarged. The term *fractal* (from the Latin word *fractus,* "broken" or "fragmented") was coined in the 1970s by French-Polish-American mathematician Benoit Mandelbrot. In 1979, Mandelbrot discovered a method of feeding the answer to an equation back into the equation that caused a computer to generate an endless self-repeating pattern. What was most noteworthy about this discovery was in the fractal's ability to repeat itself endlessly at different scales. The fractal was a geometric pattern that is infinitely self-similar at every scale.

Frenemy. A frenemy is a person or group that is friendly toward another because the relationship brings benefits but harbors feelings of resentment or rivalry.

Grace. The expression of the unconditional love that is universal consciousness. Grace is love, dancing with all possibilities equally. Grace is the spinning of the torsion fields that form matter, reality, and experience. Grace is consciousness experiencing itself in the moment as flow. Grace is available to all of us regardless of whom we are, what we know, what we have experienced, or what we feel worthy of receiving. Grace is a freely available currency of potential that reconfigures us in every moment. Grace blankets us unconditionally, as a permeating thread woven into the fabric of love inherent in everything. Grace heals, transforms, transmutes, and transcends all circumstances. Grace is ever present and abundantly available to us all. Grace is the calm-unity in community. Grace is knowing without knowing how we know. Grace *is* love. Grace is the space where anything can happen. Grace is the cohesive, invisible container that unites morphic fields with the unified field of consciousness potential.

Graceholder. Describes the transformational process that occurs through letting go of attachments and expectations in relation to placeholders. When a placeholder becomes a graceholder, the pattern no longer holds the same place in our reality. We become present to the grace and gift of the moment in total self-love as completion.

Heart-centered awareness. A state that enables us to access our core essence as unconditional love. Heart-centered awareness naturally enables us to transcend the perceived limitations of duality. There is nothing to do, and *no-thing* to compare. Heart-centered awareness taps into a well of limitless information and energetic potential. It embodies the space of all-inclusion and personal power because it evokes the knowledge that there is nothing over which to exert power.

Heartist. Who we are when we live from our hearts first and allow the mind to follow. This includes the heArt and Science of heart-centered awareness.

Heart-field. The field of the heart is a tube torus comprising two torsion fields. Torsion fields are spiraling antennae that send and receive information to and from the body, as well as to and from the environment. The torsion fields of the heart-field resemble a doughnut comprising two counterrotating fields, with the inner torsion field spinning in one direction and the outer torsion field spinning in the opposite direction. Within these torsion fields, there is a vortex, or a still point. Within the vortex, information as potential couples with both of the enfolding torsion fields. This creates a certain amount of inertia and momentum simultaneously, which helps the information pop through this vacuum as form, action, and experience. Information (inform-in-action) as possibility creates experience directly from the field of the heart. When we access the field of the heart, we access pure potentiality *prior to* that potentiality expressing as form and experience. One reason we drop down into the field of the heart is because it allows us to access a state of pure potentiality and neutrality. From the field of the heart, we can access undifferentiated states of information and consciousness potential *before* the information separates into form and defines itself through action, perspective, and/or experience.

Heart–mind synthesis. Utilizing the gift of the heart's intuition and the gift of the mind's logic together for a powerful synergy that provides for *anything-is-possible* living. Heart–mind synthesis is the integration of heart-centered awareness, coupled with the intellect, providing for choice with discernment.

Heart-prints. New maps created through the coordinates of heart-centered choices. They are like footprints for the soul. This integrative language of heart-centered awareness coupled with the power of congruent choices creates indelible imprints, heart-prints that pave the way for the Integrity Effect to ripple into our personal and collective realities.

Heart-terms. Conditions that are established by our True Authentic Self through heart–mind synthesis based on coherent connection to the field of the heart. These are the conditions we are aligned with and willing to have participate in our lives.

Holodeck. In the fictional Star Trek universe, a simulated reality facility located on starships and star bases. In this book, a holodeck is a virtual reality simulation of various possibilities that we can run in our mind's eye through our Love-sphere. Each simulation has its own set of features, benefits, probabilities, and potential outcomes. By running a holodeck in our Love-sphere, we can form useful references and distinctions in our awareness that become available to us for manifestation and decisions. Holodecks also serve as placeholders for past and future reference.

HoloFractal. *Holo* means that the whole is represented within all points within a certain system. *Fractal* means that the same basic pattern is repeated on all scales This means that all of the coordinates we map from our hearts, the various ways of relating from our hearts, always occur from a space of wholeness and completion.

Holo-frame. A framework for relating to ourselves and others from a space of completion. This includes self in relation to placeholders.

Hologram. A hologram is a three-dimensional image created with photographic projection using a laser. A hologram is produced when a single laser light is split into two separate beams. The first beam is bounced off the object to be photographed. Then the second beam is allowed to collide with the reflected light of the first. Where the two laser beams intersect and create an interference pattern is captured on film. When the film is developed, the picture is indiscernible to the naked eye. It looks like fuzzy overlapping waves or ripples in a pond. However, when the film is illuminated by another laser beam, a three-dimensional image of the original object appears. The characteristic of a hypothetically perfect hologram is that all of its content is contained in any finite part of itself, albeit at lower resolution. In other words, holograms contain all the information needed to reconstruct a whole image. Contrary to regular photographs, every part of the hologram is an exact reflection of the whole. The hologram has the entire information system for the complete image programmed into every piece of it and contains many dimensions of information in far less space. The whole of the image is in its parts.

Holographic universe. The essence of the holographic paradigm is that there is a more fundamental level of reality beyond what is visible, an invisible reality that is inherently interconnected and perpetually in a state of flux. In a holographic paradigm, nothing is separate. There exists a reciprocal enfolding and unfolding of patterns of information amid the flux, or holomovement. All potential information amid the universe is holographically encoded in the spectrum of wave patterns we may resonate with, connect to, and experience.

Holonomics. The science of integration. Derived from the Greek word *holos* (global) and *nomos* (natural laws), the term *holonomics* refers to the investigation and application of the principles that apply to integrated systems. Holonomics researches the connective network that unifies all entities under a common model of interaction and exchange. It constitutes an empirical approach for the understanding of living systems, their interaction with the environment, and their continuation in life. The fundamental understanding of holonomics asserts that everything exists in a context of interconnection and meaning. It considers that for every existing system, "the whole is greater than the sum of its parts," meaning that the whole comprises a pattern of relationships that are not contained in the single parts but ultimately define them.

Horizontal awareness. A limited framework for seeing reality from a lateral surface level through the framework of fragmentation. Seeing through a lens of predictability based on what has happened in the past. Perceiving a problem, situation, or circumstance through the limited perceptual filters with expectations.

Individual, individuality. Our uniqueness. Individual (in-divide-u-all) and individuality (in-divine-duality) refer to our unique experience of ourselves, not as separate and apart from universal consciousness, but as direct extensions of it. We are all unique expressions of universal consciousness, and we all stem from that which includes all identity.

Inductive logic. Considered the opposite of deductive logic. Inductive reasoning makes broad generalizations from specific observations. In this type of reasoning, we may make observations and distinctions, or discern a pattern and then make a sweeping conclusion.

Infinite potential. Unlimited possibilities and expressions; without limits or boundaries.

Informal logic. Mode of logic used in everyday reasoning and argument analysis. Informal logic consists of two types of reasoning: deductive and inductive.

Information (inform-in-action). Information, as potential, is stored within consciousness containers known as torsion fields. Information resonance establishes a connection to the information, activating its potential, and what is expressed is energy and experience.

Informational field. A morphic field of information as potential. (*See also* Morphic field)

Integrity. Integrity is authenticity. Nothing to fear. Integrity is not some external standard that is incessantly beyond reach. Integrity is within us, and is not something to earn. Like grace, it is freely available if we choose. Integrity is simply being wholly (who we truly are) without identifying ourselves exclusively through the masks and personas that we may hide behind. Authenticity is not so scary. Many spend their whole lives running from themselves and hiding inherent greatness behind projections. Waking up to being exactly who we are, with total acceptance, can stop the exhausting marathon of avoidance. In the pause, if only for a moment, there is a meeting of the soul as our unique sole signature begins to express in an entirely new and liberated way. It becomes like breathing. Easy. Integrity, as authenticity, brings forth joy from within. Nothing to do other than to be. Integrate (In-to-great), and express from that natural whole state. Integrity is also the expression of coherence and congruence in all intentions and actions. Integrity is a presence of heart and mind that responds honestly in the moment to *what is* with full transparency. We make a powerful choice when we embrace integrity. When we embody integrity, coherence invariably follows, as they are not mutually exclusive. Integrity establishes a coherent field of connection with all that is, allowing for all that we already are to unfold into all that we are meant to become.

Integrity effect. Extraordinary living and manifestation; a consequence of embodying heart-centered awareness and True Authentic Self, characterized by coherency, congruency, and integrity in action.

Interactive reality creation. The process of actively participating from the heart and mind through heart–mind synthesis to create and manifest experiences.

Joy. An ever-present essence that is found through the heart's inherent connection to universal consciousness. Joy is available to us regardless of our circumstances. Joy is our natural state of being. When we embody a present state of joy consistently, joy shimmers, a brilliant trans-lucence in the intersecting waves of our reality.

Knowingness. Knowing without knowing how we re-ally know; trust as a timeless transformative treasure. Heart-centered awareness is a knowing without know-ing how we know. This knowingness expands our aware-ness from a prison of limited intellect to a prism of in-tuitive, inherent, and infinite intelligence. Knowing now without knowing how we know; to know, to choose, and to experience from the field of the heart is the presence of knowingness. (*See also* Intuition)

Left brain. The logical part of the brain that compart-mentalizes and segregates information. This part of our awareness separates, and labels reality. (*See also* Right brain)

"Let go into the gap and notice that the gap is no longer there." When our heart's desire and its outward manifestation are similar, the gap between them is no longer there. The gap can be a placeholder in our aware-ness, marking our progress and movement toward de-sired experience. Awareness of the gap can be a marker for consciousness, showing us that, because we are in perpetual motion, we are never stuck. When we let go into the gap, we create a bridge from our heart's desire to its manifestation. We let go into realizing we already are what we wish to become.

Letting go. Also known as surrendering or allowing. Al-lowing provides for a return to flow. When we allow for change, which is our natural essence, then change be-comes an allowance for unlimited potential. Letting go is a liberation of attachments to *what is* and *what seemingly is not*. Letting go is an embrace with the all-inclusive; it embraces everything. Inclusion is freedom that has no opposite. It simply *is* and *is not*, together, as one. When we allow, embrace, and include everything, we have no need to hang on to anything.

Leverage. A trajectory or marker in our awareness allowing for personal evolution, transformation, or coherence within a unified field so we may witness the unfolding of something different. (*See also* Wiggle room)

Logic. A tool to develop reasonable conclusions based on a given set of data. Logic is free of emotion and deals very specifically with information in its purest form.

Love. Love is All. All is Love. Love IS. (*See also* All)

Love-sphere. Rather than dropping into your heart, allow your heart-field to surround you as a clear, transparent sphere. I refer to this as a Love-sphere. This Love-sphere is an exterior construct representing heart-centered awareness and the counterrotating torsion fields which intuit information. It is your own personal reality bubble of love. This Love-sphere can expand or constrict according to your preference. As a clear bubble of unconditional love, the Love-sphere can serve as your atmosphere for being in the heart-field and navigating through the world from a space of completion. This is one of my favorite ways to play with being in the heart and living as my own heartist.

Manipulation. Twisting love and siphoning it off into a constrictive funnel called *agenda*. Clear the agenda. Love is free of agenda. Manipulation is a method of using love to suck power. Manipulation creates a power struggle and a drain on our resources.

Maps. Models that explain consciousness. Maps expand our experience of ourselves as limitless beings. Maps are tools for navigating through all the patterns of consciousness.

Mask. A form of projection we habitually wear when relating to others and also to ourselves. Masks are a choice, not a must. Most people, though, are not aware that their masks are not who they are. Masks do not ultimately define us or limit us, unless we let them. Any representation of ourselves that is not who we truly are in our essence is a mask. Some masks are useful personas that help us navigate effectively through experiential reality, especially *in relation to* others. Masks limit us when we identify with them, that is, when we think the mask is who we are instead of simply a chosen container of consciousness expression we step into that extends from our True Self as no-self to that which is the all. When a mask becomes a permanent fixture of our self-projected awareness, we may lose sight of who we truly are. All masks are constructs. Masks by themselves are not inherently good or bad. Some masks are useful, and some are not so useful. Being able to notice our masks while retaining the essence of our True Authentic Self is the difference between experiencing rigidity, limitations, confusion, and dis-ease vs. leveraging masks for greater flexibility, expansion, clarity, and well-being.

Miracle. Any occurrence that is outside the realm of expectation or beyond preconceived notions of what is likely to occur. When we let go of expectations, preconceived notions, and attachment to specific outcomes, then every moment is a miracle unfolding. When we expect the unexpected, the unexpected soon becomes the new normal. Miracles are consciousness potential unfolding through us, as us.

Morphic field. A term coined by biologist Rupert Sheldrake in his *Hypothesis of Morphic Resonance*. It is a field within and around a morphic unit that organizes its characteristic structure and pattern of activity. Morphic fields underlie the form and behavior of holons, or morphic units, at all levels of complexity. The term *morphic field* includes morphogenetic, behavioral, social, cultural, and mental fields. Morphic fields are shaped and stabilized by morphic resonance from previous similar morphic units, which were under the influence of fields of the same kind. They consequently contain a kind of cumulative memory and tend to become increasingly habitual.

Morphic resonance. As defined by Rupert Sheldrake: "The influence of previous structures of activity on subsequent similar structures of activity organized by morphic fields. Through morphic resonance, formative causal influences pass through or across both space and time, and these influences are assumed not to fall off with distance in space or time, but they come only from the past. The greater the degree of similarity, the greater the influence of morphic resonance. In general, morphic units closely resemble themselves in the past and are subject to self-resonance from their own past states."

Morphic unit. According to Sheldrake: "A unit of form or organization, such as an atom, molecule, crystal, cell, plant, animal, pattern of instinctive behavior, social group, element of culture, ecosystem, planet, planetary system, or galaxy. Morphic units are organized in nested hierarchies of units within units: a crystal, for example, contains molecules, which contain atoms, which contain electrons and nuclei, which contain nuclear particles, which contain quarks."

Meme. Richard Brodie, in *Virus of the Mind*, defines a meme as "a unit of information in a mind whose existence influences events such that more copies of itself get created in other minds." He looks at memes in terms of their "catchiness" and defines the effectiveness of a meme based on how quickly the thought is replicated.

Neutrality. The state in which there is no charge on the positive or negative polarity. There is also no judgment. *What is* just *is* in its entirety. Both sides of the polarity, positive and negative, are included. Neutral resides in the space between positive and negative, and that is where things most readily change. Neutrality is all-inclusive. Neutrality does not mean not caring; it means feeling connected to everything, which means that everything is available. Neutrality creates an opportunity (portal-to-unity) for us to transcend our perceived limitations. Neutrality is an extension of oneness and provides us with the leverage for something to change. When we relate to one another, being neutral is a compassionate form of caring.

Not knowing. We can access our full potential when we move beyond perspectives of what we think we know. Rigid adherence to ideas and beliefs about anything creates limiting parameters, shrouding us from expanding into the realm of indeterminacy, where all things are possible. By opening into not knowing, we gain access to everything that extends beyond the inkling of what we know. From an expansive space of not knowing, our awareness moves from a limited perspective into that which is without perspective and limitless. Knowing nothing provides access to all.

Nucleus accumbens. Thrill signals that start in the lower brain are then processed in the nucleus accumbens via dopamine, serotonin, and oxytocin. New mothers are flooded with oxytocin during labor and nursing, supporting a strong connection to their babies. Often implicated in addiction and the processes that lead to addiction. *Dopamine levels in the nucleus accumbens rise in response to both rewarding and aversive stimuli.* The most widely accepted perspective now is that *dopamine levels don't rise only during rewarding experiences but instead rise anytime we experience something that can be deemed either positive or negative.*

One. All. Love IS.

Pattern. Information contained in a specific configuration, which, through resonance, is expressed as energy and experience. Our experience of reality is a result of our resonance with patterns of information. Labeling a problem as a pattern or placeholder allows us to move our awareness into neutral territory. Furthermore, it provides us with wiggle room to reconfigure the pattern. Interacting with a *pattern,* rather than a *problem, condition,* or *disease,* also frees that pattern from its morphic and memetic resonance with other similar patterns. (*See also* Placeholder)

Pebble dropping into a pond. A metaphor to describe our perceived personal reality. The pebble represents our choices. The pond represents the universe. Choosing to drop a pebble into the pond creates a ripple effect that emanates in all directions, reverberating through everything related to your choice. The pebble creates the ripples. In turn, the ripples respond to our pebble. (*See also* Ripple effect)

Perfectly imperfect. Describes the experience of the True Authentic Self (TAS); the experience of existing peacefully within oneself as a limitless being with perceived limitations. It is totally perfect to be perfectly imperfect. (*See also* True Authentic Self)

Personal power. A function of grace, personal power is not power over anything or anyone. As defined in this book, personal power is power that comes from direct access to the field of the heart and from the infinite potential that is available when we plug into the grid of universal consciousness potential. A heart-centered connection is not about having power over anyone or anything.

Perspective. A single point of reference.

Physics of heart-centered awareness. Torsion field physics that support action-at-a-distance, remote healing, instantaneous healing, time-travel, levitation, invisibility, and unlimited (free) energy. The physics of torsion fields is an emerging model that seems to explain what has been going on for thousands of years. It is the physics of us. It is the physics of love.

Placebo effect. The measurable, observable, or felt improvement in health or behavior not attributable to a medication or invasive treatment that has been administered. It suggests that one can treat various ailments by using the mind to heal.

Placeholder. In mathematics, a placeholder is a symbol used in a logical or mathematical expression to represent another term or quantity that is not yet specified but may occupy that place later. So the placeholder is something used or included temporarily, or a substitute for something that is not known or must remain generic— it is that which holds, denotes, or reserves a place for something to come later. $x = 3$, x is a placeholder, an unknown number as part of the equation that sums to the whole. *Placeholders are often used to describe part-to-whole relationships.* Placeholders literally and energetically hold places in our awareness. A placeholder may be anything in our personal perspective reality or collective consciousness to which we are relating in our lives. A placeholder may be a thought, emotion, problem, condition, filter, mask, or habituated behavior. Limitations as placeholders may resemble problems, conditions, and diseases. A placeholder may also be an opportunity, possibility, or potentiality not yet expressed. A placeholder may be a person, archetype, structure, or resonant morphic field. Anything and everything in our lives can be a placeholder for reflection. All placeholders to which we are relating may be representations for self-love as reflective awareness or the perceived absence of self-love. As there is no external substitute for the inherent love that we are, all placeholders with which we resonate may serve as mirrors, shining back to us an aspect of ourselves we may not yet recognize, accept, integrate, transcend, or transform as part of our inherent wholeness. (*See* http://www.collinsdictionary.com/dictionary/english/placeholder)

Play. A state of being that has no agenda but to joyfully engage with the moment and notice what we notice.

Play puts us in our hearts and enables us to bypass our linear, logical, analytical brain, which constructs our reality based on what is familiar. Play is the portal to freedom of choice; it offers the ability to respond to our circumstances instead of reacting. PLAY is Potential Love Awaiting You to join in the fun. Choose to play. Just play!

Possibility states. The transient unfoldings of our limitless potential *prior to* its actualization as experience. Possibility states surround us in every moment.

Practicality. The state of being practical, as applied to the aspects of a situation that involves the actual doing or being experience of something, rather than theories or ideas about it.

Practically perfect. The practice of being and experiencing what already is perfect. Practically perfect does not mean *almost perfect* or *not quite perfect*. Practically perfect is the practice of recognizing the inherent perfection in everything.

Practical play. M-Joy approach to everything that is universal consciousness. Everything is practical. Everything is play.

Problem. Defined by *Merriam-Webster's* as "a matter or situation regarded as unwelcome or harmful and needing to be dealt with and overcome." This predominantly negative personal perception sees certain matters as being in our way, which limits our options. On a polarity scale, a problem gets a negative charge. The unknown solution for an identified problem would sit on the opposite end of the polarity scale, yielding a corresponding positive charge. Unfortunately, as long as we are attempting to focus on finding a solution for a problem, we are resonating with its polarity, and that is the problem.

Projection. We may come to know ourselves through the reflections of others. When these reflections from others are not accurate, we can forget who we truly are. When these reflections are projections of distorted perceptions, we may encode information that does not match our limitless essence.

Protection. Defense against perceived harm or loss. When we are in a reality subset that says we need protection, we can know that our perception needs protection, too. As long as we *believe* we need protection, we need protection. The perceived need for protection is a matter of resonant vibration. Where we resonate, so we shall experience. Love needs no protection. Awareness of love is protection. Sometimes love wears a raincoat or camouflage to get through a storm or jungle. Awareness is key. Protection is simply an extension of awareness. If you perceive a need for protection, see yourself inside a Love-sphere and invite that bubble to expand to include everything you notice.

Questions. Questions are the answer. The answers are within the questions.

Reality. We can never definitively know what reality is. We can know reality only through how we perceive it. Our lens of awareness provides us with a mechanism for noticing, perceiving, and experiencing something we call reality.

Relating. A dynamic, ever-evolving essential of relationships. Relating is us *in relation to*—everything!

Resonance. Vibration. Resonance is connecting to a specific pattern of information that creates a template for experience. Resonance is synchronizing awareness to a particular configuration of consciousness. Resonance is established through the power of choice. Being aware of different resonant realities through information dissemination is what empowers us to make choices.

Rheomode. Physicist David Bohm proposed a new mode for utilizing language which he called the *rheomode*, from the Greek *rheo-* (to flow). His feeling was that language should reflect movement, flow, and continual transformation. He felt that language was far too object oriented or noun based and was causing us to see the world as static images. Therefore he proposed that language should focus on verb-based terms reflecting movement along a continuum rather than on object-oriented, fixed nouns. Bohm felt that a movement of language in flow reflected the deeper underlying order of interrelatedness and interconnectedness of everything in the implicate order.

Ricochet Effect. A consequential out-loop of supporting individuals, groups, structures, and circumstances that lack integrity. The Ricochet Effect occurs as a result of our willingness to show up to help others, and the result brings forth negative circumstances for ourselves. The support ricochets back and hits us in myriad harmful ways.

Right brain. The intuitive part of our brain. The right brain is a parallel processor that is able to track multiple waves of possibilities simultaneously. The right brain can track patterns of information as probabilities *before* they are actualized. The language of the right brain is symbolic and pattern-oriented. It can track connections that typically are not captured by the segregating, serial processing of the left brain. The right brain appears to be governed by waves of interconnecting grids of possibilities. When we drop into our hearts and expand our awareness into a state of playfulness that has no expectation, agenda, or attachment to an outcome, when we expand beyond what we expect to see and beyond thinking, then we enter into the domain of right-brain awareness. (*See also* Left brain)

Ripple effect. Refers to the inherent connectivity of everything. In the earlier metaphor about dropping a pebble into a pond, the pebble represents your choices. Wherever you drop a choice into the pond of universal consciousness, it creates ever-expanding ripples that spread in all directions, reverberating through everything directly or indirectly related to your choice. The ripple effect also applies to transformation and love. The ripples of the universe respond to your choices. The ripple effect is the holographic placeholder for your interactive reality creation. The ripple effect applies to everything that is related to you. (*See also* Pebble dropping into a pond)

Schema. A cognitive framework or mental concept that helps us organize and interpret information. Schemas can be very useful because they allow us to rapidly interpret vast amounts of information in our environment. However, these mental frameworks also cause us to exclude pertinent information and to focus instead only on things that confirm our preexisting beliefs and ideas.

Search. Awareness expressing through our curiosity, synchronized with infinite potential.

Secondary gain. Motivator, conscious or unconscious. Within strategy memes and association memes, often there are secondary gains with which we resonate either consciously or, more likely, unconsciously. Continuing to run a program or hang onto a pattern may be due to a secondary gain. Remove the secondary gain and the pattern often falls away.

Selfish and *Self-is*. Loving self is not selfish. Our True Authentic Self (TAS) knows this truth. Rather, we might call it *self-is*, because the TAS recognizes self as a direct extension of love. Moreover, self-care is a potent carrier wave for joy. Appreciating ourselves honors our needs and desires in myriad ways. It amplifies love, and more love becomes available for others. There is nothing selfish in loving self.

Spirituality. Spirituality means something different to everyone. Many define spirituality as the search for something sacred outside the domain of the physical world.

Supirituality. A superior (somewhat) smug stance taken by anyone who purports to definitively know what is required for any other person to evolve, transform, and ascend into a "higher" level of spiritual progression. This includes the trend toward categorizing what is spiritual versus what is not, light worker us-versus-them mentalities, and the excessive use of the term *spiritual bypassing* for any experience that appears not to involve pain, struggle, and many years of concerted effort and time.

Sympathy. An affinity between people or things in which they affect each other. An inclination to think or feel like another. Energetically, sympathy is entraining oneself to another's resonant vibration. Practically speaking, when another is miserable and we sympathize, we are likely to become miserable, too.

Synchronicity. According to Carl Jung, "synchronicity is the coming together of inner and outer events in a way that cannot be explained by cause and effect and that is meaningful to the observer." When we are thing and recognize that there is no such thing as coincidence.

Synthesis. According to scientist Dr. Carl W. Hall, "synthesis is a way of thinking and doing, of providing a vision, in which an idea or a thing, imagined or real, is seen as a coherent whole; often consisting of parts, from which thought can be developed, action can be rejected or taken, and the thing made, assembled, or constructed; either as a new creation or activity or as a duplicate or substitute of known substances."

TAS commitment vows. Our most important intimate relationship is the one we have with ourselves. It is you *in relation to* you, an eternal marriage between your True Authentic Self and your heart. The vows are simple, profound, and meaningful. Commit to love, honor, and listen to yourself through your heart, in sickness and in health, for richer or poorer, in death you won't part. Vow to appreciate, encourage, and support yourself when you need it most, and even when you do not need it. Promise to always be honest with yourself and to express your truth as it occurs to you. When you forget any of these promises, remember the premise of forgiveness, as forgiveness is an ever-evolving gift of grace. Find your joy in this marriage with yourself. Be joy. Live joy. In-Joy! Love self first and foremost, and from there, love exponentially. Love is the ripple effect.

Time. According to *Merriam-Webster's Dictionary,* "a nonspatial continuum that is measured in terms of events which succeed one another from past through present to the future."

Time as torsion. In 1913, Dr. Eli Cartan was the first to demonstrate clearly that, in Einstein's general theory of relativity, the flow of space and time not only *curves* but also possesses a spinning or spiraling movement within itself. This is known as torsion. It is generally accepted that the space surrounding Earth, and perhaps the entire galaxy, has what is called *right-handed spin.* This simply means that energy is influenced to spin clockwise as it travels through a physical vacuum. This torsion research was expanded by the work of Nikolai A. Kozyrev in Russia. Using rotation and vibration in laboratory experiments, systematic research was able to demonstrate that it is torsion fields that influence the flow of time.

Torsion. Spin.

Torsion field. The quantum spin of empty space, the large scale coherent effects of the spin of the particles in the virtual sea. Torsion fields appear to be everywhere in the universe and are forms of subtle energy. A torsion field is also known as a *spin or field, axion field, spin field,* and *microelectron field.* In the 1920s, Albert Einstein and Elie Cartan did initial work in this area of study, which is now known as the ECT (Einstein–Cartan theory). On a macroscopic level, torsion fields are generated by classical spin or by the angular-momentum density of any spinning object. The spinning of an object sets up polarization in two spatial cones, corresponding to a left torsion field and a right torsion field. At an atomic level, nuclear spin, as well as full atomic movements, may be the source of torsion fields, which would mean that all objects in nature generate their own torsion fields. These fields are not affected by distance; they instantaneously spread out through space; they interact with material objects by exchanging information; and they explain such phenomena as telepathy and photokinesis.

Torsion field physics. An emerging model of science that studies torsion fields. It is also known as scalar physics.

Torus. A unique form of flow in hydrodynamics, a torus allows fluids to spiral inwards and outwards on the same surface of the torus. It is a very stable flow form. If the universe is essentially created from one universal substance, the ether, it must be form that is used to create different and separate things out of this universal substance. The torus is nature's perfect-flow form for creating in the formless ether a seemingly separate entity that is stable enough to last. Everything is formed through the torus. The heart-field is a torus. The torus is the container through which consciousness expresses itself as matter, form, and experience.

Transcend (trance-end). To rise above or go beyond, overpass, or exceed is the general meaning. In this book, to transcend means to move beyond a limited construct of consciousness into a new form of information expression, energy, and experience.

Transcending (trance-ending) duality. The experience of recognizing that duality is part of our experience but does not limit our experience. This is also referred to as unity consciousness.

Transform (trance-form). To modify the form or expression of something. Our essence as limitless beings is a constant that does not change. Our experience or expression of that essence is the process of change experienced through transformation.

True Authentic Beauty (TAB). Inner radiance that wells up from the field of the heart and shines throughout the physical body temple. Translucent brilliance of TAS that is a unique expression of universal consciousness and infinite potential. No comparison. Only completion.

True Authentic Desire (TAD). Genuine desires that well up from the field of the heart. True Authentic Desire is a cue from universal consciousness to pay attention, for when allowed to unfold, TAD manifests as magnificence. TADs are feeling states that are not characterized necessarily by emotions or logic. Rather, they are an inner knowing. TAD is a knowing what we know without knowing how we know. TAD can be most readily accessed and expressed when embodying True Authentic Self (TAS) and in True Authentic Relating (TAR).

True Authentic Opinion (TAO). An expression of True Authentic Self that is a perspective unique to every individual.

True Authentic Power (TAP). Inner strength and truth accessible through the field of the heart and grace. Nothing to power over. Inner dominion.

True Authentic Relating (TAR). The congruent expression of coherency by our True Authentic Self. True Authentic Relating is integrity in action. TAR is clear intent and right relations.

True Authentic Self (TAS). Differs from our Authentic Self, which embodies limitations. Our TAS embodies limitlessness with limitations. In effect, it says, "I know I am consciousness potential and a being without limits, and yet I coexist peacefully with my self-imposed limitations. Daily, in each moment, I am unfolding and letting go of who I was the moment before so that I can embrace more of who I am becoming." Our TAS has presence and awareness of divine being, which is unconditional love in the form of coherent light. It also has limiting self-concepts that have been conditioned into personal awareness. These coexist and synthesize without judgment. Our TAS is willing to explore parts of the self that may not match the picture of its limitless being, opening into those parts with the same love and light. Our TAS embraces the full totality of being; it does not hide the yucky stuff from awareness. Our TAS is perfectly imperfect.

Truth. Ultimately, truth is a deeply personal experience. For the purposes of this book, truth means understanding our own truth for ourselves in regard to the nature of our own reality as a limitless being.

Two (too!). Everything *in relation to* . . . Everything is you, as One, *in relation to* an other. In relation is Two.

Unconditional love. The cohesive force that unifies all, as well as that which creates the fabric of the universe. Unconditional love is not the kind of love that we humans have become accustomed to, with all its parameters, expectations, and limitations. It is not "I love you." It is Love IS. Expressions of love, no longer unconditioned by virtue of being conditioned into an expression, are powerful, coherent placeholders for our potential return to wholeness and connection with Source as universal consciousness.

Unity consciousness. The state in which oneness and duality are perceived as an extension of unity. Duality is part of our experience but does not limit or define our experience. (*See also* Transcend [trance-end])

Ventral tegmental area (VTA). A clump of tissue in the brain's lower regions that is the body's central refinery for *dopamine*. Dopamine performs many functions but primarily regulates reward. Winning the lottery can produce a thrilling rush of dopamine.

Vertical awareness. An expansive holonomic framework for seeing reality through love's completion. Beyond predictability. Bird's-eye timeless perspective.

Vortex. A little eddy or tornado that draws everything that surrounds it into its powerful current.

WE experience. Balanced living with an equal emphasis on service to self and service to others. The WE experience is more than uniting with others in the name of community. The role of the individual in the true WE experience is not diminished for the overall whole. Rather, the role of the whole individual is pivotal and is directly proportional to the role and value of community cohesion.

Wellness. Health. A natural flow that is expressed through a body of information that serves as a vehicle for consciousness. Thus, wellness, or well-being, is a conditioned expression of consciousness and love flowing through form from its original unconditional state. Ultimately, well-being is consciousness potential expressing itself as love and light through us. Focusing on well-being without trying to be well or to avoid disease allows our natural state of flow to well up and reverberate from the core of our being. When we let go, we are in flow. Wellness or well-being is a matter of conditioning consciousness. Condition yourself to be free from your conditions. Energetically align awareness to focus upon where you want to be, so that form and function may follow.

Whole. The essence of that which we are. Complete.

Whole-brain thinking. Integration and synthesis of both the left and right hemispheres of the brain. Consider that the left brain–right brain dichotomy is more myth than fact. This persistent belief stems from research done by Roger Sperry and Mike Gazzaniga in the 1960s. However, current neuroscientific research reveals that function is not tied to a specific area of the brain or hemisphere.

Rather, function is a distribution network of cells spanning the brain across lobes and *both* hemispheres.

Wiggle room. Leverage. Information noticed within a pattern that offers the greatest degree of flexibility to unravel a pattern and create a different configuration. A perceived opening into a different possibility, noticed beyond the current experience. Movement of awareness through a rigid construct to create greater flexibility, expansion and flow. Wiggle room is what we notice, or perceive, when interacting with patterns that have been defined as problems, conditions, or disease. Wiggle room can be identified by asking an open-ended question such as, "If I knew where the *wiggle room* is within this pattern, so that the pattern could change, what might I notice?"

You. Complete. All. I AM. Love. Unique. Present to show the universe something it has never seen before.

Zero. A placeholder.

Zero-point energy (aka Zero-point field). Quantum science in the twentieth century revealed the presence of an all-pervasive background sea of quantum energy in the universe. Cambridge University's Dr. Harold Puthoff was one of the first to measure this energy. He measured it at zero degrees kelvin, the absolute lowest possible temperature in the universe, which is equal to minus 273 degrees Celsius. According to Newtonian physics, at this temperature all molecular and atomic movement should have ceased that is, no energy should be measured at all! Instead of finding no energy, as expected, Dr. Puthoff found what he called "a seething cauldron" of energy; henceforth, it was given the name zero-point energy. Puthoff proved that the physical vacuum is not at all devoid of energy and that, instead of being a vacuum, space is actually a plenum. Princeton University's John Wheeler and Richard Feynman were the first to value the zero-point energy. They calculated that a cup of zero-point energy is enough to bring all the oceans of the world to the boiling point. Contrary to what we have always believed, matter is not a condensed substance but a diffuse form of energy. The field of the heart gives us direct access to the Zero-point field. The Zero-point field is also considered consciousness potential.

Notes

Chapter 1
1. http://www.yourdictionary.com/concrescence.
2. http://science.jrank.org/pages/3035/Germ-Theory.html.

Chapter 4
1. "A History of the Heart," https://web.stanford.edu/class/history13/earlysciencelab/body/heartpages/heart.html.
2. Rollin McCraty, Raymond Trevor Bradley, and Dana Tomasino, "The Heart Has Its Own 'Brain' and Consciousness," *in5d* (blog), January 10, 2015, http://in5d.com/the-heart-has-its-own-brain-and-consciousness/.
3. Barbara Tversky and George Fisher, "The Problem with Eyewitness Testimony," *Stanford Journal of Legal Studies* 1, no. 1, https://agora.stanford.edu/sjls/Issue%20One/fisher&tversky.htm.
4. *Collins Dictionary,* s.v. "placeholder," http://www.collinsdictionary.com/dictionary/english/placeholder.

Chapter 5
1. https://www.brainyquote.com/quotes/authors/a/anais_nin_2.html.
2. https://www.scribd.com/document/333396046/Logic.
3. Alina Bradford, "Deductive Reasoning vs. Inductive Reasoning," *Live Science,* March 23, 2015, http://www.livescience.com/21569-deduction-vs-induction.html.
4. "What Is Logic? Definition and Examples," http://study.com/academy/lesson/what-is-logic-definition-examples-quiz.html.
5. https://www.mrc-cbu.cam.ac.uk/people/matt.davis/cmabridge/.

6. Kendra Cherry, "What Is a Meme in Psychology?," Very Well, June 22, 2016, https://www.verywell.com/what-is-a-schema-2795873.

7. M. R. Westcott, in a report on intuitive thinking at Psychology of Intuition, New York, 1968.

8. Kayt Sukel, "Can We Quit It with the 'Right Brain, Left Brain' Stuff Already?," http://bigthink.com/world-in-mind/can-we-quit-it-with-the-right-brain-left-brain-stuff-already.

9. Zhenghan Qi et al., "White-Matter Structure in the Right Hemisphere Predicts Mandarin Chinese Learning Success," *Journal of Neurolinguistics* 33 (2015).

10. Karl H. Pribram, "Holonomy and Structure in the Organization of Perception," in *Images, Perception, and Knowledge,* ed. John M. Nicholas, 155–85 (Dordrecht, Netherlands: D. Reidel, 1977), http://www.karlpribram.com/wp-content/uploads/pdf/theory/T-095.pdf.

11. W. J. Long, "Quantum Theory and Neuroplasticity: Implications for Social Theory," *Journal of Theoretical and Philosophical Psychology* 26 (2006): 78–94.

12. Cited in Chris Renzo, "Neuroplasticity and Its Implications for Human Potential," *Waking Times,* October 27, 2012, http://www.wakingtimes.com/2012/10/27/neuroplasticity-and-its-implications-for-human-potential/.

Chapter 6

1. Alanis Morissette, https://www.brainyquote.com/quotes/authors/a/alanis_morissette.html.

2. "Emotional Intelligence," Psychology Today, https://www.psychologytoday.com/basics/emotional-intelligence.

3. Julie Beck, "Hard Feelings: Science's Struggle to Define Emotions," *The Atlantic,* February 24, 2015, http://www.theatlantic.com/health/archive/2015/02/hard-feelings-sciences-struggle-to-define-emotions/385711/.

4. William K. Larkin, "Thoughts or Feelings? Which Comes First?," *Applied Neuroscience* (blog), http://appliedneuroscienceblog.com/thoughts_or_feelings_which_comes_first.

5. "Feeling Our Emotions," *Scientific American,* https://www.scientificamerican.com/article/feeling-our-emotions/.

6. Lynn Grodzki, "Approaching a Theory of Emotion: An Interview with Candace Pert, PhD," http://www.primal-page.com/pert.htm.

7. Bhavika, "Alter Your Genes and Cure Any Disease," *Fractal Enlightenment* (blog), https://fractalenlightenment.com/.../alter-your-genes-and-cure-any-diseas...

8. *Oxford English Dictionary*, s.v. "empathy."

9. Richard Jenkins, quoted in John Rapaport, *The Secret behind Secret Societies* (Escondido, CA: Truth Seeker, 1998).

10. Kendra Cherry, "What Is the Superego?," June 5, 2016, https://www.verywell.com/what-is-the-superego-2795876.

Chapter 7

1. "Know Your Brain: Nucleus Accumbens," June 13, 2014, http://www.neuroscientificallychallenged.com/blog/2014/6/11/know-your-brain-nucleus-accumbens.

2. Jeffrey Kluger, "The Science of Romance: Why We Love," *Time*, January 17, 2008, http://content.time.com/time/magazine/article/0,9171,1704672,00.html; Therese J. Borchard, "The Science of Romance: The Love Drug," *World of Psychology* (blog), https://psychcentral.com/blog/archives/2011/02/11/the-science-of-romance-the-love-drug/.

3. S. Thobois, E. Jouanneau, M. Bouvard, and M. Sindou, "Obsessive-Compulsive Disorder after Unilateral Caudate Nucleus Bleeding," *Acta Neurochirurgica* 146, no. 9 (2004): 1027–31.

4. https://theanatomyoflove.com/the-results/ventral-tegmental-area/.

5. Nicole M. Avena, "Food 'Addiction': Translational Studies of the Fine Line between Food Reward and Addiction," talk presented at the ILSI annual meeting, 2016.

6. Ibid.

7. "Study: Sugar Hidden in Junk Food Eight Times More Addictive Than Cocaine," ABC News, February 25, 2015, http://abc13.com/health/study-sugar-is-as-addictive-as-cocaine/533979/.

8. Sean Coughlan, "Facebook Lurking Makes You Miserable, Study Says," BBC News, December 22, 2016, http://www.bbc.com/news/education-38392802.

Chapter 8

1. http://www.azquotes.com/quote/318154?ref=integrity.

2. Jocelyn Voo, "How Birth Order Affects Your Child's Personality and Behavior," *Parents*, http://www.parents.com/baby/development/social/birth-order-and-personality/.

3. *Merriam-Webster's Dictionary*, s.v. "collateral damage."

Chapter 9

1. http://www.sheldrake.org/research/glossary, emphasis added.
2. Ibid.
3. Sheldrake, *Dogs That Know When Their Owners Are Coming Home* (New York: Broadway Books, 2011), 305.
4. Sarah Knapton, "Patients on Antidepressants for 50 Per Cent Longer than in 1990s," *The Telegraph,* January 15, 2017, http://www.telegraph.co.uk/science/2017/01/15/patients-antidepressants-50-per-cent-longer-1990s/.
5. Brendan L. Smith, "Inappropriate Prescribing," *Monitor on Psychology* 43, no. 6 (2012), http://www.apa.org/monitor/2012/06/prescribing.aspx.
6. "Depression Drug (Benzodiazepines, SNRIs, TCAs, TeCAs, Atypical Antipsychotics, Monoamine Oxidase Inhibitors and Others) Market: Global Industry Perspective, Comprehensive Analysis, Size, Share, Growth, Segment, Trends and Forecast, 2014–2020," http://www.marketresearchstore.com/report/depression-drug-market-z53043.
7. Omudhome Ogbru, "Antidepressants (Depression Medications)," http://www.medicinenet.com/antidepressants/article.htm.
8. "The Chemical Imbalance Theory—Officially Proven False!," http://www.anxietycentre.com/anxiety/chemical-imbalance.shtml.
9. http://www.ssri.news/.
10. Clare Wilson, "High Antidepressant Use Could Lead to UK Public Health Disaster," *Daily News,* May 12, 2016, https://www.newscientist.com/article/2087949-high-antidepressant-use-could-lead-to-uk-public-health-disaster/.
11. http://media.aace.com/press-release/american-association-clinical-endocrinologists-aace-and-american-college-endocrinology.

Chapter 10

1. https://www.brainyquote.com/quotes/keywords/synthesis.html.
2. Daniel J. Ott, "Process Communitarianism," *Concrecence* 10 (2009): 67–75.
3. "Lisa Randall, "Knocking on Heaven's Door," lecture at Harvard University, November 2011, https://m.youtube.com/watch?v=FiCNLZMhScI.
4. "Looking for Extra Dimensions," http://www.superstringtheory.com/experm/exper51.html.

5. "SpaceTime, Relativity, and Quantum Physics," http://www.ws5
.com/spacetime/.

6. Dennis Overbye, "On Gravity, Oreos, and a Theory of
Everything," *New York Times,* November 1, 2005, http://www
.nytimes.com/2005/11/01/science/on-gravity-oreos-and-a-theory-
of-everything.html.

7. The field of the heart enables us to access the hidden additional
dimensions beyond 5-D, such as 6-D, where the morphic field
imprints for 3-D may rest; 7-D of sound; 8-D of light, and so on.
Barbara Hand Clow and Gerry Clow, *The Alchemy of Nine Dimensions*
(Charlottesville, VA: Hampton Roads, 2010).

8. David Yurth, *Seeing Past the Edge* (Mesa, AZ: Dandelion Books,
1997); Richard C. Hoagland and David Wilcock, "The Bees' Needs:
It's the Physics, Stupid!," http://www.enterprisemission.com/Bees/
thebeesneeds.htm.

9. Vladimir Poponin, "The DNA Phantom Effect," http://www
.soulsofdistortion.nl/dna2.html.

10. Carl W. Hall, "The Age of Synthesis," *The BENT of Tau Beta Pi,*
Summer 1997, https://www.tbp.org/pubs/Features/Su97Hall.pdf,
emphasis added.

About the Author

Melissa Joy Jonsson (M-Joy) is an author, a speaker, an inspirational leader, and founder and instructor of "M-Joy" seminars. She is best known for her ability to engage people from all over the world to embrace their True Authentic Power by playing in the field of the heart. She has a unique perspective on how we are able to experience living joyfully and loving completely.

Melissa has been teaching popular life-transformational seminars around the globe since 2008. In 2014, she launched the "M-Joy" seminar teachings, a unifying WE movement in consciousness dedicated to heart-centered awareness and practical personal empowerment for everyone. Melissa's teachings are a culmination of her expansive work integrating scientific principles and spiritual concepts into practical daily experiences. She provides a new language to experience self-love as integrity.

In addition to *The Integrity Effect*, Melissa is the author of several best-selling books, including *Little Book of Big Potentials: 24 Fields of Flow, Fulfillment, Abundance, and Joy in Everyday Life* (2015) and *M-Joy Practically Speaking: Matrix Energetics and Living Your Infinite Potential* (2014). She also authored *Practical Play the Heart-Centered Way: A Complementary Play Guide to Little Book of Big Potentials* (2016). Melissa coauthored, with Dr. Richard Bartlett, *Into the*

Matrix: Guides, Grace, and the Field of the Heart (2013) and *The Physics of Miracles: Tapping in to the Field of Consciousness Potential* (2010).

Melissa Joy is passionate about inspiring every other person to realize his or her True Authentic Self (TAS) with practical, creative, and powerful wisdom.

To learn more about M-Joy, please visit http://www .MJoyHeartField.com/.

Made in the USA
San Bernardino, CA
23 August 2017